RAISING THE
DEAD

ALSO BY

Richard Selzer

Down from Troy

Imagine a Woman

Taking the World in for Repairs

Letters to a Young Doctor

Confessions of a Knife

Mortal Lessons

Rituals of Surgery

THE GRAND ROUNDS PRESS ®

RAISING THE DEAD

Richard Selzer

WHITTLE DIRECT BOOKS

The Grand Rounds Press®: Martha Hume, Senior Editor; Ken Smith, Design Director;
Hillari Dowdle, Associate Editor; Susan Brill, Associate Art Director

Library of Congress Catalog Card Number: 92-62301

Selzer, Richard
Raising the Dead
ISBN 1-879736-11-X
ISSN 1053-6620

The Grand Rounds Press

The Grand Rounds Press presents original short books by distinguished authors on subjects of importance to the medical profession.

The series is edited and published by Whittle Books, a business unit of Whittle Communications L.P. A new book is published approximately every three months. The series reflects a broad spectrum of responsible opinions. In each book the opinions expressed are those of the author, not the publisher or advertiser.

I welcome your comments on this unique endeavor.

William S. Rukeyser
Editor in Chief

In laying myself down like ash after the flame
Have I surrendered?
No, I am sleeping and despite night's power
Learning like a child that I shall awake.

—Paul Eluard

part *one*

I T WAS IN AUGUST OF THE YEAR 1810 THAT FANNY D'ARBLAY (née Burney), an Englishwoman living in Paris and the most famous woman novelist of her day, experienced for the first time "an annoyance" in her right breast. Pressing her hand against the discomfort, she felt within its substance a hard lump. For several minutes she reconnoitered with her fingers, then dismissed the finding from her mind. She would not think about it. But the pain would not be dismissed. Within weeks, what had begun as an occasional twinge became a heavy ache from which she was rarely free. Still, out of fear—some might call it ignorance—Fanny continued to deny its importance to herself as well as to her much concerned husband, Alexandre. Obstinately, she deflected his entreaties to see a surgeon. Months went by during which the tumor enlarged and the pain intensified. At last, Fanny's repugnance for a physical examination was overcome. She would, after all, be examined. It was Dubois, the most celebrated surgeon of France, who was summoned—he, because once before she had been his patient for the successful treatment of an abscess. Dubois looked and palpated and gave the dreaded news that an operation would be necessary but that, having recently been appointed *accoucheur* to the pregnant Empress Josephine, he would not be free to return until the empress had been safely delivered. Fanny was, by now, distraught. Another name was suggested, that of Dominique-Jean Larrey, chief surgeon of the French army and favorite of Napoleon. Having distinguished himself during the military campaigns in Egypt, Poland, and Austria, Larrey had been rewarded with the title of baron by a grateful commander in chief. It was said that Larrey had once cured a Polish woman of a similar malady without surgery.

More terrifying than her pain or the obvious growth of the tumor was the prospect of an operation, for which Fanny's horror was insuperable. To be held down, screaming, and cut open like a melon! Send for Larrey, then, she said at last. But the surgeon proved to be a reluctant consultant, unwilling to attend her until a letter had been sent by Fanny to Dubois explaining that her severe fright and continued pain made it impossible to endure the delay occasioned by the royal confinement. Larrey had no wish to make an enemy of the great Dubois. With the receipt of that letter and the consent of Dubois, the case of Fanny d'Arblay was made over to Larrey.

From the first visit, Larrey became the repository of Fanny's fairest hopes. A nonsurgical regimen was recommended: compresses, diet, unguents, and rest. Relief at having escaped the knife and some fortuitous lessening of her pain conspired to form Fanny's opinion that her new doctor was the "most singularly excellent of men, endowed with real Genius in his profession." Her sharp novelist's eye also took note of his "ignorance of the world and its usages" and of a certain naiveté that, to the unfamiliar, might give him the appearance of being simple and even weak. "But they would be mistaken," Fanny wrote in her diary. It is only that "his attention having been turned exclusively in one way, he is hardly awake in any other." Over the year of their relationship as doctor and patient, Fanny and Larrey were to conceive the warmest friendship for each other. This was to the great benefit of Fanny, who surrendered herself with full trust to his ministrations, but it may have cost Larrey, who was seduced by his charming and vivacious patient into stripping off the protective carapace that is necessary to any man whose work it is to lay open the bodies of his fellow human beings.

In the weeks that followed, Fanny noted an upswing in the level of her energy. With the lessening of the pain, real or imagined, and no further increase in the swelling, the lesion had appeared to halt its advance and even to show signs of subsiding. Although she still had "cruel seizures," they were shorter and less frequent. Fanny responded with optimism, declared herself better in every way. She was able to go out every day and to receive friends at home. Larrey shared her relief and pronounced himself "enchanted" at her improvement, though apparently not without some misgivings, as he insisted on another opinion—that of Ribes, the first anatomist of the nation—lest his own "excessive desire" to spare his patient the agony of surgery had deluded him. To Fanny's joy, Ribes concurred with Larrey's conservative treatment.

What, then, was Larrey's consternation when he returned at the beginning of September 1811, a year later, to find a marked worsening in the condition of the breast and a deterioration in the patient's general condition. Not only had the swelling advanced, but Fanny's right arm had become useless because of the pain. She required the help of a maid in order to dress. Why had she not summoned him earlier?

"*Et qu'est-il donc arrivé?*" he cried. "What is going on here?" The tumor could not be dissolved, he told her sadly. Surgery would be necessary. Once again Ribes was called in. Once again he concurred, corroborating the bad news. Though she could no longer even climb a flight of stairs without suffering, Fanny, terrified, pleaded for time. A third doctor, the physician Moreau, was summoned. Might he not suggest an alternative? But Larrey had tried everything already. On the day of Moreau's visit, Larrey and Ribes were also present. Together, all three doctors condemned the patient to the operation that she feared more than death itself. With nowhere to turn, Fanny was trapped. Calling up all her reason, if not her courage, she acquiesced. Not all of her anguish could keep her from seeing the tears in the eyes of Larrey. Would she like to be seen by Dubois once more? he offered. Touched by this expression of modesty, Fanny rejected the offer. No, she told Larrey. If she could not be saved by him, she had no hope elsewhere. But now it was Larrey's turn to plead for time. She should obtain the best advice in France, he told her. She was too esteemed, too valued. "The public will be outraged if . . . if . . . you have not the best we can offer you." Perhaps, he said, Dubois might even now suggest a cure without surgery. At that, Fanny was won over. Send for him! Send for him! she cried. But Dubois, fully occupied with his other patients, was not immediately available. He would come as soon as he could, and, furthermore, he would inform her of the date only on that very same day in order to avoid further agitation.

When the time came at last, after a nightmare of waiting, there were four doctors in the salon of the house on the rue de Miromesnil outside of which, with sublime indifference, Paris went on being Paris. Once the examination had been completed, Fanny retired from the room to permit them to consult. After half an hour of torment, she was led back in for the verdict. "All were silent, and Dr. Larrey hid himself nearly behind my sofa. My heart beat fast. I saw all hope was over." It was Dubois himself, disturbed by her plight, who pronounced her doom.

"Will there be much pain?" she asked.

"You must expect to suffer," said Dubois. "I do not wish to fool you. You will suffer greatly."

Now it was the anatomist Ribes who spoke. When the time came, she must not restrain her weeping. To do so would have serious consequences. Hadn't she screamed at the birth of her son? asked Moreau. Yes, she told him. She could not help but do so. Why then, there is nothing to fear, he said. Two things more: Monsieur d'Arblay must not be at home during the time of surgery, and Fanny would not be informed of the date until a few hours ahead. It was the one measure they could take to relieve her anxiety, by shortening its worst period.

And now it was the last day of September, thirteen months since her discovery of the tumor. At 8 a.m. a letter was delivered by a young surgeon, Aumont. In it Larrey wrote that he would arrive at 10 a.m., properly accompanied. He charged her to arrange by whatever subterfuge that her husband be made absent from the house. He exhorted her to rely on his dexterity and experience. Two hours! Larrey again explained that he had deemed it wise to give such short notice to spare her anxiety. With her husband standing by the bedside, Fanny read and reread the letter, her mind darting to think of some ruse by which d'Arblay might be sent away. With all her heart, she wanted to spare this "most loving of men" the sight and sound of her ordeal. Dismissing him momentarily, she sent a note to his employer imploring that an urgent summons call her husband to business and that he be detained until all should be over. That done, Fanny, ever mistress of her household, stifled her fear and told the young surgeon Aumont that she would not be ready until one o'clock. She needed three hours to prepare an apartment for her banished mate; there were nurses to engage, a bed, curtains, heaven knows what, to prepare. Under no circumstances would she be ready until one o'clock. Aumont refused to leave the house and remained in the salon cutting and folding into bandages and sponges the old, fine, castoff underwear he had requested.

At one o'clock, another message came: M. Dubois could not come until three o'clock. Now Fanny, with nothing further to prepare, had only to think and pace. The sight of all those bandages and compresses made her ill. Back and forth, from room to room, she toiled, stilling herself by force of will until she was nearly "torpid."

At last, the clock struck three. There was the clatter of many hooves on the rue de Miromesnil. Fanny raced to the window and saw the cabriolets— one, two, three, four—roll up in quick succession to halt at her door. From each carriage one or two sober-faced men were discharged. With a particular shudder, she recognized Larrey, the man who would, before the hour was up, take up his knife and lay open her body. She retreated to her room. A moment later, the door was opened and seven men in black entered the bedroom of Fanny d'Arblay. It was indignation that roused her from her stupor. Why so many? And without leave! But she could not utter a word of objection.

Once inside, it was Dubois who acted as commander in chief, ordering a bedstead to be placed in the middle of the room, demanding two old mattresses, an old sheet. Fanny was astonished. A bedstead! When Larrey had assured her than an armchair would suffice. She turned to him for confirmation but Larrey kept himself out of sight, at the periphery of the hubbub, his head downcast, his eyes averted. Fanny felt herself trembling, losing control of her nerves. The operating theater having been arranged to his satisfaction, Dubois bid her mount the bedstead. For a moment, she had an impulse to race to the door, the window, and escape. But reason reinstated itself and she stood her ground.

"Please remove your robe," said Dubois, issuing the command *en militaire*. Her robe! She had meant to keep it on. But submit she did. Oh how she longed for her sisters, all so far away, or a friend who would protect her modesty. At the evidence of her despair, Dubois softened and spoke a few soothing words. But Fanny did not hear.

"Can you," she cried out to him, "can you imagine how I approach this operation that, *to you*, must seem so trivial?"

"Trivial?" he repeated, and in his discomfort he took up a bit of paper and tore it unconsciously into pieces. "*Oui*," he stammered, "it is a small thing . . . but . . . ," and could not go on. Somehow Dubois' agitation canceled her defensiveness. A glance at Larrey, who remained at the farthest reaches of the room, showed her a face as pale as ashes. Then Fanny knew the enormity of her danger. Unbidden now, she mounted the bedstead. Dubois settled her upon the mattress and spread a cambric handkerchief over her face—a pitiful blindfold through which she could see that the bed was surrounded by the seven men. Hands were laid upon her, to hold. Through the cambric she saw the glitter of polished steel, then closed her eyes and waited. A long silence ensued in which she imagined that the surgeons discoursed with signs. At last someone spoke.

"Who will hold the breast?" It was the solemn, melancholy voice of Larrey. No one answered. Through the handkerchief, she saw the hand of Larrey above her breast describing with his finger the lines of his incision. A straight line from top to bottom, a cross, and a circle, intimating that the whole breast was to be taken off.

Unable to keep still any longer, Fanny started up, threw off her veil, and cupping her breast from the bottom to present it to the surgeons, she cried:

"Who will hold the breast? *C'est moi, Monsieur*. I will." Swiftly and firmly Dubois replaced her as before, covering her face again with the handkerchief. Fanny closed her eyes, and waited. It was the moment of incision.

When it came, she felt the knife drawn about her breast followed by a wake of pain "like a mass of forked poniards tearing." Fanny needed no encouragement to let herself go, but heard from her own throat an animal howl such as she had not thought a human capable of, a howled vowel that was interrupted only by the need for more breath to propagate itself anew. She imagined the knife describing a curve, now cutting against the grain as the resistant flesh opposed and tired the hand of the surgeon who must again and again change the knife from one hand to the other. At last the knife withdrew. *It is over*, she thought. But no. In the next moment, the thing lowered its snout to feed again, more voraciously than ever, as it separated the "dreadful gland" from the parts to which it was adherent.

"*Ah, messieurs*," she cried. "*Que je vous plains!* How sorry I am for you!" Again a pause as Larrey rested his hand. Again the scalpel lowered, now audibly raking against her breastbone. Scraping! At last, in the midst of her agony, Fanny felt that the knife had been withdrawn from her flesh. There was a pause, after which she heard Larrey ask his colleagues "in a tone nearly tragic" if anyone saw a need to cut away any more tissue.

"Yes," came the voice of Dubois, and she could *feel* his finger pointing above the wound. The cutting resumed. Another pause. Now Moreau discerned another peccant atom. Again Dubois, demanding yet a bit more flesh. And another. Just before losing consciousness, the screaming woman cried out: "In the name of God, what are you doing to me?"

Her next memory was of being lifted and carried to her own bed. Only then did she open her eyes to see Larrey looking down at her, "pale nearly as myself, his face streaked with blood, and its expression depicting grief, apprehension and almost horror." The operation, from incision to closure, had taken twenty minutes. To Fanny it had seemed twenty years. In this account, given by Fanny nine months later in a letter to her sister, the dramatic terms in which the event is rendered are those of the novelist whose heroine is not unlike Joan of Arc. Hadn't Fanny mounted her bedstead as bravely as Joan of Arc had her stake? Hadn't she "forgiven" her surgeons much as Joan had forgiven the men who convicted her? Hadn't Cardinal Beaufort and the judges wept as they sealed the fate of the Maid of Orleans even as the surgeon Larrey's eyes had filled with tears? Her utterances themselves are those of a martyr. If no one else, then she, Fanny, would present her breast to the knife. "How sorry I am for you," she had cried. Only in her last outcry: "What are you doing to me?" is there any human spontaneity. As for the rest, they are the words of the supremely self-conscious and melodramatic novelist. One

A Shift in Perspective ...

The flexibility to shift perspective is key to creativity and innovation.
Sometimes a closer view or a different angle reveals a whole new truth.
Sometimes it takes a step back to see the larger picture. At Marion Merrell Dow
we are committed to an ongoing effort to discover, explore, and deal with
reality by looking at our world from various and differing points of view.

MARION MERRELL DOW INC.

hastens to forgive her entirely for her self-indulgence.

In the postoperative report, written the next day by one of Larrey's pupils, we read:

> At 3:45 on September 31, 1811, Mme. d'Arblay submitted to the removal of a fist-sized cancer that originated in the right breast and was adherent to the pectoralis major muscle. The operation was performed by M. le baron Larrey, assisted by Professor Dubois and Drs. Moreau, Ribes, and Aumont. It was very painful and endured with great courage. The center of the tumor showed early cancerous degeneration, but all its roots were excised, and in no other case has so serious an operation promised more hope of success.
>
> The extreme sensibility of the patient caused the most violent postoperative spasms which were only controlled by the use of sedatives. The patient had an uncomfortable night—full of agitation, spasms, headache, nausea, and vomiting. . . . But by ten in the morning the patient was astonished to find herself alive and fairly comfortable. Upon his arrival, M. Larrey found her to be without fever, and with very little pain and virtually no bloody drainage. . . .
>
> He prescribed cream of rice soup and a jelly of meat. Also, chicken soup and a decoction of thickened barley water with lemon. This evening she took a second decoction of linseed and the flower heads of the poppy.

Although nothing in the scanty report indicates the nature of the incision, the type of sutures, or the measures used to control bleeding, it is possible to infer what took place from what is known of Larrey's technique as it is described in his *Memoirs of Military Surgery*. The incision may be assumed to have been of the simple guillotine, or circular, type, as was used in the performance of so many amputations on the battlefield. Surely, this would have been the quickest way to remove the breast. In the absence of anesthesia and in the desire to cause as little bleeding and surgical shock as possible, speed was essential. Larrey was known to have amputated a shattered arm or leg in three minutes from the incision in the skin to its closure without sutures. In any operation, only the largest of the blood vessels were ligated with waxed cotton thread, the rest being allowed to stop of their own accord by clotting, or by use of cautery with a hot iron. To close the wound, flaps of skin with its underlying fat would have been undercut, loosened, and lifted to meet similar flaps from the opposite margin. The edges of apposed skin would then have been sutured. But loosely, with gaps left between the stitches to allow for egress of blood, serum, and any tissue injured or destroyed during the procedure, and above all, to allow for the release of pus. To Larrey, as to all other surgeons of his time, the sight of pus streaming from a wound forty-eight hours after surgery was cause to rejoice, as it meant that in all likelihood, the underlying tissues were healing. Pus to these surgeons was "laudable." They gave thanks for it. Suppuration having been established, one had only to wait for new tissue to build up from the base of the wound and for the skin to grow across the separated edges. Any more meticulous approximation of the wound would surely serve to seal in the inevitable pus and invite complete breakdown of the wound or worse: blood poisoning and death.

The diagnosis was cancer of the breast. From the beginning, Fanny had experienced pain, heaviness, and tenderness. Within months the function of her arm had become impaired so as to keep her from dressing herself or writing. In time, she could not climb a flight of stairs without exhaustion. The mass was visibly and palpably enlarging. At the time of the surgery, it had reached the size of a man's fist. Moreover, it was noted to have extended into the muscles of the chest. What else could it be but a cancer?

It is not to take away from Larrey's singular achievement—only twice before, in 1655 and again in 1718, had mastectomy been performed for what was thought to be cancer of the breast—nor to demythologize Fanny's novelistic account of her peril that one must, in retrospect, have some reason to doubt the accuracy of the diagnosis. Fanny d'Arblay lived for twenty-nine years after her operation, surviving both her husband and her son. It is unlikely that so locally extensive a cancer would have been eradicated by an operation that did not include removal of the lymph nodes under the arm. Although such a large and longstanding cancer might have remained confined, it is more apt to have broken out of its bounds and spread via the bloodstream or the lymphatic ducts to distant parts of the body.

What else might it have been? A chronic, indolent abscess—syphilitic, tubercular, or otherwise bacterial—can by compression of the adjacent tissues produce about itself a hard, fibrous capsule that would give the mass the feel of a solid tumor when in fact it is a cavity containing liquid or semisolid material, such as is described in the operative report. Such an abscess would excite in the surrounding tissues an inflammation which would cause the lesion to adhere to the underlying chest wall so as to give the impression of tumor extension when it might have been no more than inflammatory tissue. A chronic abscess of this type could produce infected lymph glands in the armpit and so give rise to pain in the arm itself. Against such a diagnosis is the great age of the lesion, at least thirteen months. By then, an abscess could be expected to have produced redness and swelling of the skin. The natural course of such a lesion is to grow ever more superficial until at last it bursts forth to the outside.

Another, more likely diagnosis is cystosarcoma phyllodes, a usually benign tumor that can grow to great size before stabilizing. It is not unheard of for such a tumor to grow so quickly that it outstrips its own blood supply and undergoes necrotic degeneration at its core. Here too, the inflammatory response could produce adherence to the chest wall. The pain in Fanny's arm could have been referred from the breast via the branches of the brachial plexus of nerves in the armpit. Against this diagnosis is Fanny's age, 59, far older than most, but not all, women who develop this benign tumor.

Fanny d'Arblay had been a literary lioness, admired by Samuel Johnson, Edmund Burke, Thomas Macaulay, and Jane Austen (who took the title of her book *Pride and Prejudice* from Fanny's novel *Cecilia)* for over a quarter of a century, since the publication of her first novel—*Evelina*, the story of a young girl's entry into English society—in 1778. Each of her novels was awaited as impatiently as those of Sir Walter Scott. Throughout her life she moved in brilliant aristocratic circles both in her native England and in Paris, where she lived with her French husband, Count Alexandre d'Arblay. It was enough to turn any writer's head. And it did.

From her voluminous diary, it is not hard to form the portrait of a vain, opinionated woman with an insatiable appetite for compliments, yet vivacious, witty, effusive to the point of hysteria, shallow but never insincere, and with an immense gift for friendship. And with a novelist's eye for detail. In her own eyes, she was saintly, just, affectionate, and too often victimized by the less high-souled and the jealous. To the historian striving for impartiality, she emerges as a difficult but fascinating woman with a kind of full-dress elegance, understandably adored by her less flamboyant husband and son, about whom she orbited like a luminous moon. A woman who grew, not up, only older.

How far from the unvarnished facts the novelist strayed in the recapitulation of her martyrdom one cannot, and would not, say. Such ignoble doubting is for the cynics of medicine and literature, of whom there is no lack. The only account was written in a letter to her sister nine months after her surgery. How far, after all, from the facts of the Passion of Jesus Christ are the much delayed writings of Matthew, Mark, Luke, and John, each of which differs significantly from the others? Besides, what writer has not overshot a mark or two in his time? History is as much a matter of opinion as it is of fact. Whatever else is open to question in the case of Fanny d'Arblay, her suffering is most emphatically authentic. What happened, happened. A woman had a tumor of the breast. A surgeon removed it without anesthesia. The woman was cured.

And what of the surgeon Larrey? With tears in his eyes and a face "pale as ashes" at the thought of the suffering of his patient? Could this be the first surgeon of the French army who at age 45 had already accompanied Napoleon on his campaigns to Egypt and Syria, Austria, Poland, and Spain? Who had, with legendary courage, performed thousands of operations on the field of battle amid showers of bullets and whirlwinds of snow and sand, often with no more shelter than a cloak held over the patient by two men during the procedure?

Of a surgeon it is said that he is but an extension of his scalpel, a man whose emotions must be held prisoner in the deepest compartment of the heart lest he be unmanned and his resolve fail him. As this is not true of the majority of surgeons (women, now, as well as men), it was not true of Larrey. So unblunted was he, even in the midst of the calamities of war, that he was unable to refrain from tears at the screams of the wounded and the misery of the soldiers which it was not in his power to alleviate. Possessed of genius himself, Larrey worshiped genius in others, whether it resided in a famous woman writer or in Napoleon Bonaparte, whose exile on Elba he was only deterred from sharing by Napoleon's insistence that he remain with the army of France.

Months later, in the new intimacy between Fanny and Larrey born out of the shared experience of having gazed together into the mouth of hell, Larrey was to reveal to Fanny d'Arblay that he too had all but lost his nerve. It seems that at the time of the last consultation, Dubois had declared the lesion inoperable, the cancer too far advanced for surgical removal. Any operation could only hasten her death. At that moment, Larrey, in the words of Fanny, "regretted to his soul ever having known me, and was on the point of demanding a commission to the furthest end of France in order to force me into other hands." Hyperbole? Perhaps, but entirely forgivable in the convalescent's portrayal of her ordeal and rescue. It is a small pleasure considering the suffering that went before. It is a pleasure of which few patients hesitate to avail themselves. "Mine," a visitor is told, "was the largest kidney

A Shift in Perspective...

Work Locally...

A Shift in Perspective Makes a World of Difference

Work Locally but Think Globally

Around the world, Marion Merrell Dow research centers are home to hundreds
of physicians and scientists whose curiosity and joy of discovery are nurtured
in an atmosphere of freedom, openness, and informality. In Cincinnati, Kansas
City, and Indianapolis...in Strasbourg, France and Gerenzano, Italy...in
Winnersh, England and Hirakata, Japan—local Marion Merrell Dow associates
look for innovative approaches and new perspectives in pharmacology.
At each local facility, the view is global.

MARION MERRELL DOW INC.

stone my doctor had ever seen." That sort of thing.

Larrey died at the age of 72, two years after the death of Fanny d'Arblay. It is one of those ironic judgments of history that Larrey, the surgeon, was to outlive Fanny, the novelist, in the matter of literary reputation as well.

With the arguable exception of her first novel, *Evelina*, the rest of her literary output, hugely popular in its day, has not stood the test of time. It is undistinguished, some say unreadable, and justly forgotten. Whereas the military and surgical memoirs of Baron Larrey are masterpieces of medical history, rendered in prose so meticulous and sharp as to suggest having been written with something other than a pen. A scalpel, perhaps? Here he is on the treatment of frostbite during the campaign in Russia:

> It will easily be conceived why, instead of submitting the part to heat which provokes gangrene, it is necessary to rub the affected part with substances containing very little calorie. Snow and ice are the substances to which recourse should be had. Should this fail, the part ought to be plunged in cold water until bubbles of air are seen to disengage themselves from the congealed part. This is the process adopted by the Russians for thawing a fish. If they soak it in warm water, they know from experience that it will become putrid in a few minutes; whereas, after immersion in cold water, it is as fresh as if it had just been caught.

Now show me the writer who wouldn't die to have written that.

◆

In 1624, the poet John Donne, vicar of Saint Dunstan-in-the-West, took to his bed with a grave illness that brought him to the verge of death. A precise diagnosis was never made, although the disease was characterized by fever, rash, and cough. Most likely were two possibilities: typhus or so-called relapsing fever, both of which have been indicted as the cause of the epidemic fever that swept London in 1623 and 1624. The acute illness lasted about three weeks, presumably the length of time needed for the disease to burn itself out. Donne himself survived and went on to contract tuberculosis two years later, and cancer of the stomach some six years after that. During the acute illness, Donne jotted down notes that described his spiritual reactions to his physical state. These later formed the basis of his *Devotions Upon Emergent Occasions*, twenty-three sets of prose pieces, each consisting of a prayer, an expostulation, and a meditation. Taken all together they constitute a spiritual quest inspired by a dangerous illness. In writing of their illnesses, Fanny d'Arblay was the consummate storyteller making the literary most of what happened to her; John Donne was the philosophic divine, seeking the meaning of affliction.

Now it would seem only natural that a convalescent scrivener, having survived his own dangerous illness, should attempt to follow in the footsteps of two such eminent writers. But I did not share Madame d'Arblay's charming yen to make romance out of life. And long years of skepticism have distanced me from prayer and expostulation, both of which imply a presence that will respond. That leaves meditation, the only category that needs no one but the narrator himself. And so I shall begin to meditate.

part *two*

❧

ON THE EVENING OF MARCH 31, 1991, IN THE HOUSE ON ST. RONAN Terrace, I sat writing in the room I call my scriptorium. Usually, in Connecticut March is winter hanging by a thread, but this year it had turned hot without any transitional period of moderation; the leaves were already half-size. For most of the month I had been on an extended lecture tour that took me from the island of Kauai to Nova Scotia, then on to Delaware, California, and Texas. Around nine o'clock I left my desk and went to stand at the open window. The branches had begun to stir in a sudden breeze. There was the muffled sound of thunder. Jagged nerves of lightning leaped. In the sultry air the pattern of the wallpaper turned from green to gold; the figures in it grew wavy, they vibrated like heat rising from a pavement. All at once, my legs buckled. From downstairs Janet heard the thud and came running.

"What?" she said.

"I can't think why . . . ," I replied.

"Can you get up?" I tried but could not.

"You'd better call . . ." But she had already dialed. Within minutes two young men in uniform stood over me. I remember being bundled up, the stretcher sliding home aboard the ambulance. One of the men took my pulse and blood pressure, then relayed the information to someone over the phone. I heard the sirens.

"For goodness' sake, don't use the sirens," I told him. "It will disturb the neighbors. Besides, it isn't that serious."

"Take it easy, Pops," said the young man. "It's sporty this way." I remember nothing else until twenty-three days later when I woke up on a ship, I thought; somewhere off the coast of Texas, I thought. Oh yes, there was this: at the emergency room I was placed on a stretcher. All around and above me, a flock of white birds—stooping to peck at my arms, groins, beaking my mouth, rectum, everywhere. Then nothing . . . save for whispers crowding around, leading me deeper and deeper into the darkness. Then they too vanished.

Coma is the state into which he is tumbling. Moment by moment, there is a turning inward of the senses. The sounds, smells, sights, perceptions of the outside world are disappearing. The Milky Way roars across the sky like an army of light. At last, his fall is broken by a soft cushion and he is suspended in a viscous, pearly matrix that is itself both time and space; his vertebrae have melted; he lies here strewn, submerged.

I feel ashamed to pounce upon the page with a narrative that is so open, explicit, so personal. In one sense it is a vivisection, the cutting up of a living creature to see how it works, rummaging among the still-quivering flesh for its soul. As you can see, I am warming up before making a start, rubbing my hands together to summon up courage. If I have written much of it in the third person, well, that is because such an obsessive account of an illness forces one, like Dorian Gray, to confront his own "devilish, furtive, ingrown" self-portrait. The pronoun *he* gives a blessed bit of distance between myself and a too fresh ordeal in which the use of *I* would be rather like picking off a scab only to find that the wound had not completely healed. Still, *I*, the author, will be present throughout, looking on, translating for *him*, the patient.

In writing this journal, I had no overriding wish to educate myself in the subject of Legionnaires' disease, the diagnosis ultimately given to my ailment. Once I had learned that it is caused by the bacterium *Legionella pneumophila*, which thrives in the mist sprayed from air-conditioning ducts, that a building or an airplane having been infested, travelers are especially vulnerable, that it is quite often a massive pneumonia associated with collapse of the respiratory function and therefore fatal; once I had glanced at a few colored photographs of autopsy specimens of lungs and liver and kidney, my curiosity about the disease was exhausted. A writer, like an old-time doctor, prefers impressions to facts. Impressions are what last. Facts, such as the data read from the screen of the computer, have a tendency to change from day to day. But I think it is time to get on with the chronicle of an illness told afterward.

Let us look in upon that cubicle of the emergency room. The stretcher upon which he lies is engulfed in nurses and doctors, each of whom is ministering to him at the same time. In a moment, his clothing is stripped from him. Because he is flailing about, his wrists and ankles have been restrained. From veins in his arms and groins endless ribbons of blood, dark from the cyanosis, are pulled into tubes. His head is steadied, his neck extended by mighty hands; the mouth of the man is pried open and an attempt is made to insert a tube into his trachea. But his agitation is extreme, like that of a man drowning. Or rather, that of a man playing the role of someone drowning in an old-fashioned melodrama. It has that jerky, staccato rhythm. Because of this, the intubation cannot be carried out. Medication is injected into a vein and the doctor at the head of the stretcher tries again.

There. Now the tube is in his trachea, the cuff inflated to keep it from slipping out. Still not fully narcotized, the man shakes his frantic head from side to side, refusing what has been thrust in. He coughs, strains, his neck is a contraption of taut tendons and engorged veins. To the uninitiated it might seem a kind of molestation. At last the morphine reaches his brain; he subsides into flaccidity. His chest lifts, recedes, lifts again at the insistence of the rhythmic, squeezing fist of a perfect stranger. Ointment is squeezed from a tube into his eyes, and his lids are taped shut to protect the corneas. It is the beginning of a long sleep. In the meantime, a catheter has been slid into his bladder, another plastic tube into one of his nostrils to gain access to his stomach. Already, long strings of blackish bile are staining the sheet on which he lies. The cardiogram shows the rhythm of his heart to be precarious—ventricular tachycardia. Drugs are administered, electrodes readied to apply to the chest. An X-ray is taken; one of the doctors remarks that the chest is not expanding symmetrically. The diagnosis is massive bilateral pneumonia with toxic shock. How strange that he had no earlier warning. Despite the administration of pure oxygen, his lips and fingernails remain blue. His temperature, they say, is very high. His pulse too, his blood pressure almost unobtainable. Is he going to die? No one knows. But there is more than a hint of death here.

Within minutes, then, he is a preparation, something they have made and whose every flicker and seepage can be measured precisely. In addition to the doctors, nurses and technicians, I, the author, am also there standing, or rather, hovering bodiless above and to the side, out of the way yet able to see, to hear, now and then able to reach down if I wish and touch him, the one lying there on the stretcher who seems to me a small bird perched on an arrow that has been shot from the bow and is flying somewhere. If ever the man wakes up and can speak for himself, I shall have to change pronouns.

The martyrdom of the intensive care unit has begun. It has a certain relentless monotony which would render any such narrative boring. So I shall not proceed day by day through the pestering and goading of the flesh that go by the name intensive care. Suffice it to say that for the next twenty-three days the man in the bed is to be ventilated, dosed, defibrillated, probed, suctioned, and infused. Most of his bodily functions will be taken over. No longer need he swallow, chew, inhale or exhale, cough, urinate, defecate, clear his throat, maintain acid-base balance, cogitate, remember, sigh, weep, laugh, desire. Even the need for making tears has been taken over by the ophthalmic ointment that protects his corneas. For those who will tend him, he is at once the raison d'être and the predicament from which they long to extricate themselves. The doctors are earnest and tireless. They remind me of poor farmers who, year in and year out, turn with their hoes the same exhausted patch of soil, planting and replanting, flogging it, cherishing it. But there will come the day when the pathetic patch of dust will no longer yield. Only then will they let it be. In other words, this man is half-dead, although not quite at the point of no return. For him death would certainly be much easier to achieve than life. The prospect of life regained is like sitting down to a gourmet lunch without the blessing of appetite.

The intensive care unit suggests a blockhouse, a building made of concrete, designed to withstand attack during wartime. Even the patient who is conscious exists here in a kind of reverie. Within the blockhouse twenty respirators, each inhaling and exhaling at its own pace, make a steady, wet noise like the fall from a fountain. Such a sound goes unnoticed in an intensive care unit beneath the clatter and thump, the footfalls, the calling out, the moaning. So cleverly has the noise of these respirators been woven into the larger fabric of sound that within minutes it cannot be dissected and analyzed for itself. Absolute silence could not be deeper. All the while, in the chimney of his brain, thoughts fly up and, a moment later, waft away, irretrievable.

Dreamer that he is, even in the blockhouse, even from the depths of his coma, he invites the IV pole, the respirator, the whole massive bank of machinery to suggest the background for a story: the hanging bottles of saline become a crystal chandelier; the moans of his sick neighbor are the sound of an oboe being played in another part of the house; the cooing of pigeons on the window ledge becomes the rapturous cries of lovers. Those who enter and leave his room will be characters in a story—there is a nurse, Maureen, with a long, slender neck at the hollow of which rests a tiny gold cross. A chambermaid performs her futile acts of domesticity, fitting her mop in and around the legs of the others. Now and then, she will cast a glance at the wreckage in the bed and sigh. Even to death and beyond, he will be the teller of tales, collecting impressions, defying forgetfulness, and meeting gods all along the road, the way you do when reading Homer or Virgil. He can do all that? In coma? Oh yes, he can. Dream, imagination— these are the chariots that the comatose body rides. It is by these that the

Beyond Science and Technology...

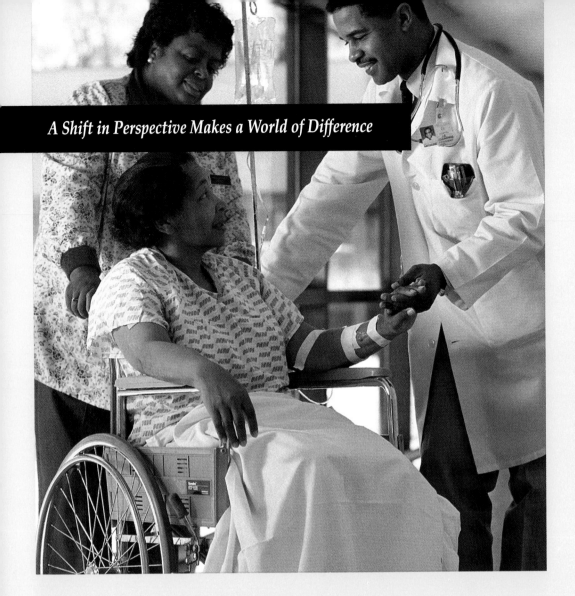

A Shift in Perspective Makes a World of Difference

Beyond Science and Technology...
Our Vision Is of Humanity

Wherever our research takes us, we never lose sight of its ultimate goal—
improving the human condition. Alleviating pain and suffering. Improving the
quality of life. Enabling the disabled. Extending the span of health and vigor.
When we look at a molecule, with a shift in perspective, we see a human being.

MARION MERRELL DOW INC.

flesh extends itself to encompass the whole world.

He had always been thin—a parcel of bones really, stitched together with ligament, strung with nerves and tendons, and with a cap of aluminum hair; his eyes are of that indeterminate color called hazel. But now it is the sixth day. He is swollen like a toad, his flesh cold and soggy, his edematous eyelids at half-mast. You wonder how they could have overhydrated him so. In their zeal to combat his state of shock, they have given him fifty pounds of excess glucose and saline solution. There is the sadness of a toad in his hazel eyes. The familiar landmarks by which he could once be identified are no longer to be seen: the zygomatic arches surmounting the cheeks, the iliac crests, the tapered phalanges. Where is the squarish mandible that (he has been told) gave his head the look of a Roman senator? Where, the graceful hollow above each clavicle? And all the while, beneath the deceptive fullness of edema, the wasting of his muscles goes on, the congestion of his internal organs. He has become something that even I would not want to touch. Not so the nurses— Maureen, Linda, Heather. Beautifully serene, they continue to stroke and massage him, to wipe away all stains, to bathe and dress him in clean linen To look at him today you would never guess that he is the same man brought to the emergency room six days ago and set loose at supersonic speed into the void and traveling on remote control.

At last, by the tenth day, the diuretic has succeeded in drying him out. Succeeded beyond anyone's expectations. All day and all night, the nurses have emptied the plastic collecting bags suspended from the siderail of the bed, exclaiming. The output of urine is nothing short of heroic. Within four days he has become little more than a skeleton, every bone visible and palpable— the skeleton of a child whose puberty has been delayed. At the same time, he looks ancient enough to have been mentioned in the Old Testament. Oh, let me confess it! Sometimes he seems brave and beautiful to me, although I know that I am the only one who would think so. Look at him! A sprig of chicory blooming between paving stones, indomitable.

DAY FOURTEEN. All the blood that is still in a liquid state has been drawn from his veins; syringe after syringe has glittered with it. The rest is clotted or extravasated into the tissues. Huge purpura, ecchymoses, and hematomas cover the sticks that were his arms. There is a moist rattle in the endotracheal tube. Now and then, a nurse detaches the tube from the respirator long enough to suction it clear, and then the rattle disappears for a while.

I have spent the entire day observing him. The poverty of his body, the way he shivers like a wet dog. The draining away of his flesh and blood. He is like an abandoned cottage in ruins, the eaves of his ribs overhanging the scaphoid belly. His umbilicus, that mute evidence of his ancestry, seems set directly upon the vertebral column. When the narcosis is allowed to lift, he curls up, stretches out slowly like a larva, signaling with the only sound he can make—the faint borborygmi of his bowel. At last I understand the term *embedded*, the way a fly trapped in a chunk of amber must apprehend its plight.

Beneath the sheet he is naked save for his feet, which are encased in brand-new high-top running shoes. His wife has shopped for them at the suggestion of Maureen, who is worried about foot drop. These massive sneakers hold the feet at right angles to the legs. It is ludicrous, and even the anguished members of his family—his children—cannot keep from smiling at the small boy who has taken his new shoes to bed with him.

DAY EIGHTEEN. He has been in coma for almost three weeks. What is it like? It is like being encased in a layer of wax that separates him from the rest of mankind. The outer air is a foreign element into which he is unable to break through. Nor should he try, for he could no longer breathe it in. An immense weight holds down his thin bluish eyelids. He could not have raised them. Nor does he want to. He has no need for eyes. Here, there is nothing for him to do but wait and listen to the silences rubbing against each other. Now and then there is a small shifting in the air as if far away, on another continent, a boa constrictor were slowly unwinding from a branch. Could this place have a name? Is it on any map of the world? A decision has been made to wean him from the respirator.

The narcotics and paralyzing agents have been given in lower doses throughout the night. Toward dawn he is lying in the upper berth of a sleeping car; there is no room to sit up or turn over. The train is hurtling across an endless prairie where it is always night. Once in a while the eternal darkness outside the train window is punctuated by something—a forest of bare white birch trees, a herd of cattle, only their white faces showing. A few silvery birds fly. Or are they fish streaming?

There are times when his face seems to contort into weeping; his eyes open and show themselves brimming with a molten sorrow. When it passes, the spasm, there is a relief about the diaphragm as when vomiting or sobbing stops and you can let go of yourself. This morning he even made a gesture as if to reach up and claw from him the skin of wax that is his coma. It is the same gesture made by Lazarus in the painting (School of Rembrandt) when he sits up in the tomb and begins to unwrap his cerements. But unlike Lazarus, the man in bed cannot manage it. By afternoon his arms and legs are once again flailing about, resisting. In the chart his behavior is noted as "combative." Nothing could be further from the truth. What makes him struggle so is not aggressiveness; it is desperation.

The man now is about the size of a small deer lying starved and exhausted in snow. See how he lifts his head, turns it slowly, on his face a look of puzzlement, uncertainty, as he sees me hovering in the corner of the room where wall and ceiling meet. Something passes between us—not quite speech. He opens his mouth as if to eject the tube but cannot. Then with a purposefulness that I did not think he could muster, he reaches one hand up and pulls it, coughing, choking, from his throat with the cuff still inflated. He seems surprised at what he has done, the sounds he is making.

"That was very naughty!" The nurse attaches nasal prongs to deliver oxygen to his nostrils until the doctor can come to replace the tube. Meanwhile, he is rid of the tube and struggles to extrude vowels and consonants from his larynx. Even his eyebrows take part in the effort to speak, the way they arch, lifting as if to encourage his lips and tongue. It gives his face a look of boyish earnestness. But there is no voice, only a thick, gelatinous rasp, as the vocal cords no longer approximate. Minutes later, the anesthesiologist arrives. Just in time, for the cyanosis has darkened. The wrists and ankles of the patient have been secured to the bed. The nurse holds his head as if it were the head of a statue whose sightless eyes have no pupils. The hands that grip him are hard as tongs. In the end he yields to them as though yielding to a strangler's thumbs. The endotracheal tube is replaced, its cuff inflated. The dose of morphine is increased. Immediately, his empty sockets return a gray, stony stare. He must remain paralyzed and unconscious until such time as he no longer needs the respirator. And so he sleeps on.

He is like a gardener digging in the earth who makes a decision to lower himself to the underworld. Down and down he goes, swinging from root to root. On either side, worms, rocks, gulches, darkness, eyes like panthers caught in a net of lashes, moisture dripping. Just so does he follow the mushroom scent of hell, and with each fathom grows paler, less opaque, his flesh melting—solid to liquid, until at last there will be only the vagueness of vapor. Once or twice he looks back up to see how far he has come, but the path behind has closed up, leaving no trace. He would not be able to find his way back. The thick, twisted roots have tapered into fine, hairlike rhizomes that he parts with his hand the way one parts a curtain of beads. His cheeks and arms are coated with cold moisture, more like rot than sweat. The odor of mushrooms grows heavier. Solid ropes of it slide in and out of his mouth, fill his throat. After a long time, the path widens and ends abruptly at the edge of a black river. Here he lies down, not to sleep—in this place there is no need for sleep or wakefulness. Nor is there any need to move.

DAY TWENTY. The sight of his hands is particularly sad. Those fine muscles between the metacarpal bones and in the web spaces—the interossei and the lumbricals—have atrophied; the mounds of flesh have given way to gullies. The skin is dry and as chaste and beautiful as old paper. But I remember the passion inspired by those fingers, their gifted, sly, infinitely provocative caresses and gestures. No sign of that now.

A doctor turns over first one hand, then the other, searching perhaps for a usable vein. Then he sees the elevated, dimpled scar tissue in each palm that begins to contract and draw down the ring finger. That is the Dupuytren's contracture of which the man has been inordinately proud. He never lost the chance to tell the gullible that these were the stigmata of the Crucifixion. The examining doctor makes a note to show the Dupuytren's contracture to the medical students.

DAY TWENTY-ONE. A gray dawn slides through the ill-fitting slats of the venetian blind. From the glum faces of the nurses, it is clear that in the block-house things are looking worse. Whatever fragile equilibrium between acid and base, between oxygen and carbon dioxide, between positive and negative that the doctors have managed somehow to piece together has come unraveled. All of the vital signs have taken a turn for the worse. Fever. If it goes any higher, he will burst into flames. A pair of gills would work better than his solidified, liverish lungs. Daedalus! You can make anything! How about it? A pair of gills for the man!

"Let him not die," someone murmurs. The possibility itself lowers the temperature in the room; the patient shivers. With the sheet pulled down, he looks more and more like a winter-starved deer, stricken. *Don't go! Not yet!* Who is that calling out? Then I see that it is I calling out in pursuit of myself. The sheet is drawn smooth up to the armpits (as though he could move) and tucked in under the mattress. When the nurse lets his head down, the pillow is scarcely dented by the weight of it. If someone had asked him at that moment what was his dearest wish, it would have been to lie on his stomach with his arms bracketing his head.

Day Twenty-Two. All day and night, silt has settled in his veins, turning them solid. Only the bubbles of saliva on his teeth continue to wink bravely in the light. A slow slide of clot advances through his body. It began in the venules of the arms and legs, filled the larger veins, the iliac, the inferior vena cava, flowing slowly toward the heart. By morning, it will have achieved the right auricle. A single muffled thump, and it will be hurled to the lungs. And there it will stay, hardening into a cast of the pulmonary circulation. Should he die, will I too feel the cold mud in the marrow of my bones?

Day Twenty-Three. And now it is my sad duty to report to you his death. It occurs at precisely 1:38 p.m. on April 23. He has been in the intensive care unit for three weeks and two days. From far away there comes a drumming so faint and rapid as to be unrecordable by even the most sensitive device in the room. Could it be rain? No, the sound lurches and staggers as though the drummer had slipped and lost his beat.

"Ventricular tachycardia," says the nurse and calls for the doctor. The drumming grows louder and louder until it fills the room. Then all at once it stops as though an arrow had been shot through the throat of the drummer boy. The pace of activity in the room quickens. Maureen pounds vehemently upon his chest, turns up the oxygen flow. Injections are given into the tubing, then directly into his heart (or where she surmises his heart to be), syringes full of calcium and adrenaline. Electrodes are clapped to his chest and a series of jolts delivered which cause the body of the man to jounce hideously in the bed. His lips and fingernails are a deep blue. Minutes go by. The doctor arrives.

"How long has the EKG been flat?"

"Four and a half minutes." For a while they continue their efforts, which are like a pantomime. To no avail. No amount of resuscitation has the least effect. The heartbeat is not restored. At last the efforts are discontinued. There he lies, the sheet having been thrown off in the struggle, his slight body pale, emaciated, childlike were it not for that head like a Roman senator's and his aluminum hair.

"This man is dead."

Maureen, she who had pounced upon him like a cat, jolted him with currents of electricity, seen to the injections into his very heart, sags against a wall. She has given up trying to catch his ghost, which was running away from her. He was already out of her reach and she could not pursue him further. Sorrowfully, Maureen sits by the bed recording the events in the chart, her usually strong, bold handwriting gone shaky. See how she pleats her forehead, draws in her lips, for in spite of all that she has witnessed over the years she cannot bear to be present at this. Time of death, she writes, 1:38 p.m.

It is strange, this painless death. Like stepping through a door held politely open for him. It doesn't seem right, somehow; a trivialization of the event. Death ought to be harder to achieve. Better to be hunted down, rooted out, hurting and bloody. Then death would come as a relief. It would be welcome.

◆

It is now ten minutes since the doctor's pronouncement of death. Already the man has taken on that look of dignity that the newly dead have because of their possession of secrets. Or is it that they travel in a beyond that must be entered formally? Maureen is still writing an account of the last minutes of his life, her efforts to resuscitate him—the intracardiac injections of calcium and adrenaline, the jolts of electricity delivered to his chest, the failure of the electrocardiogram to respond. Glancing up, she has noted the characteristic "settling" of his body, the fixity that is incontrovertible; she has seen that so many times. Alone in the room, Maureen pauses in her charting to wipe her eyes with the back of her hand. Bleary with tears, she does not see what I see, that a subtle change is taking place in the contents of the bed, that the utter stillness of the body has been replaced by a calmness of the flesh, that beneath the closed eyelids his eyeballs roll slowly from side to side, then dart the way fish will move in a pond. Look! He shudders as if to shake off something which threatens to cling, and tightens those eyelids; minnows of light rising in the shallows. Then he hears a wingbeat, and feels something fugitive, immaterial, a beige veil being drawn from his face, slowly at first then faster, until the final whisk is like a slap. A moment later he draws the first breath. It is a deep sigh that might be interpreted as one either of sorrow or of satisfaction, as though one precious thing were being relinquished and another embraced. The nurse's incredulous stare! Her galvanic leap to his side! He, blinking in the explosion of light. When he opens his eyes, their color has gone from the ambivalence of hazel to the jubilation of blue.

Again, a breath is drawn, and another and another. A tracing has returned to the electrocardiograph, which the nurse had not yet detached from his arms and legs. The room, which had descended into a subaqueous silence emanating from the corpse, is now fiercely active. All the machinery is back in place, chugging, vibrating, clicking, ringing. Nurses scurry, calling out to one another. They bend over the bed, coaxing, noting and recording each sign of revivification. The intravenous chandelier sends light streaming through his body until he is something radiant and glowing in the bed. From time to time, the nurses turn to look at each other, their faces swept with wild surmise. It is true! After ten minutes of certified death, this man has . . . risen. Risen! Such a word does not belong in an intensive care unit.

Now the man is coughing against the endotracheal tube, he wrinkles his forehead, tears stream from his eyes, he shakes his head slowly from side to side. It is painful to observe the resurrection of a man, to behold a log of inert flesh trying to raise itself. But the pain is all ours. He feels nothing as yet. He is like the bulb of a tulip probing the earth in which it has lain all winter unaware of its potential, without memory or hope. As we do not ascribe pain to the tulip in its rebirth so ought we not to imagine that he, the man, is torn loose and abraded.

Then he who has performed no purposeful movement in three weeks reaches up one hand and pulls the tube from his throat and mouth. And that is not all: a smile breaks upon his face, but such a smile as has never been seen on the continent of North America. And in a hoarse whisper, but plainly enough, he utters the single word: Yes.

"Did he say yes?"

"What do you suppose he means?"

"I couldn't say. Perhaps he was just answering a question someone had asked him weeks ago before he went into coma."

"Does that happen?"

"More likely it is some odd form of seizure activity."

What he means, what the nurses cannot know, is that everything begins with a yes. That is how the first two bits of energy in the universe greeted each other, collided. Boom! And yes! There was life. So it is with the resurrected. Once again his throat fills with the word until the pressure of it is unbearable and he cries out in the hoarse voice that sticks to his jaws . . . Yes! Saying yes to life, accepting once again the burden and thrill of it.

It is the next day. He lies on his back, arms and legs splayed out so as not to disengage any of the needles or tubes. Now and then, he is propped on one side or the other. What he really wants is to curl up so as to give himself a hug, to accept his own warmth. Still, on his face is a strange, far-off look, as if to say, death is easy; it is the return to life that requires courage. When a nurse comes to take his temperature, he follows her solemnly with his eyes that seem to say: I have been to the land of the dead. Do not touch me. From that moment on, his vital signs—pulse, blood pressure, temperature—are normal. His oxygen saturation, 100 percent. There is no longer any doubt that he will recover.

About the consternation of the entire medical staff, there is little to be said. The joy at his reawakening is general, but in each person it is colored with uncertainty.

"You must have been mistaken," they tell the nurses at the weekly morbidity/mortality conference. "It cannot be as you told it . . ."

"The cardiogram was flat," the nurses reply. "The pulse and blood pressure were unobtainable. What else do you need? He was dead."

"Then how . . . ?" The nurses shrug and shake their heads.

Throughout the hospital they can think of nothing else. For weeks, in the laundry, at the coffee shop, in the X-ray file room as in the morgue, every conversation will begin with the words: Did you hear . . . ? On whatever flimsy pretext, orderlies and technicians and next-of-kin will walk past the doors of the intensive care unit just to draw near to the site, each of them taking away a dollop of hope to be saved up for a rainy day. If it happened to *him*, then perhaps . . . It is as if no one who worked at the hospital could go on living without specific knowledge of the event. Just so has it swollen into a legend that even I have come to believe in time. Such is the power of literature, be it written down on paper or passed on from mouth to ear.

It is twenty-four days since the night he was taken to the emergency room, well into April. A warm day, with the sun streaming in and lighting up the wall of his room. Torpor envelops him. He hears grasshoppers. They seem to be in the bed with him, all around him, inside his chest. Yes! The noise of the grasshoppers is coming from inside his chest! He gives a soft, flannel cough and the stridulation abates. The ceiling at which he is gazing is made of squares of corkboard. Here and there the expanse of it is interrupted by the handle of an opaque glass panel that can be pulled down. Storage space. Or a hidden compartment like those in the ceiling of a ship's cabin. On board a ship you have to make use of every inch of space. He feels beneath him the gentle rocking of the sea. A coziness comes over him. He is perfectly comfortable. *So!* He thinks, *I am aboard a ship. But where? Perhaps I am in the*

South? Yes, he remembers, it is the South; he had been there recently, lecturing in Texas. That's it, Texas! Then he sees the intravenous attached to his arm and he thinks that while in Texas he must have fallen sick, that he is aboard a hospital ship in the Gulf of Mexico. Doubtless soon to be discharged, from the way he feels. So comfortable and drowsy.

From somewhere comes the music of a Strauss waltz. He lies utterly still, letting the light from the intravenous chandelier trickle onto his face and collect there in small glistening pools, while the mattress takes up the rhythm of the music, scooping, dipping, turning his all but transparent body. He has never felt so graceful, so comfortable in his own flesh. All at once he has an irresistible urge to laugh. Should you ask him the reason for his laughter he would not know, for it is unlike any laughter of his life but something with which he has been infested, a holdover from some almost forgotten glee, now become reflexive and without rhyme or reason. He hears a woman's voice calling.

"Wake up! Wake up, sleepyhead! What's so funny?" It is as though she were summoning him up from a great depth to the surface where he now floats between two sheets, his face visible only in the trough between the waves. He opens his eyes to see his wife, Janet, standing by the bed.

"For goodness' sake!" he says. "What are you doing in Texas, or off the coast of it?"

"This is not Texas," she informs him. "And this is no ship. You are in the intensive care unit of the Yale-New Haven Hospital."

"But the rocking of the waves . . ." He is not ready to give up.

"They have you on one of those newfangled mattresses that inflates here, deflates there. It's run by electricity. That way you won't get bedsores."

"How long have I been here?" It is the only thing he wants to know.

"About three weeks. Twenty-three days of coma to be exact." But he is already hurrying back to sleep.

part *three*

꧁

T HE STRETCHER BEARING HIM TO THE INFECTIOUS DISEASE WARD LEAVES
the intensive-care unit amid the applause and hoorays of the staff.
Maureen stays with him until she is satisfied that he has been safely ensconced in his new room. When it is time for her to go, she roughly
scrambles together the bright mane of her hair, then bends to kiss his cheek.

"You," he whispers, "all by yourself are enough to raise the dead." She lets
out a whoop of laughter.

The ward to which he has been moved is occupied by other very sick
medical patients, most with AIDS. The staff are largely Irish, brought to
America because of the nursing shortage. They are men and women whose
polite manners, wit, and soft brogue lend to the ward an atmosphere of
old-world gentility. He, however, is to be psychotic for a time—the insan-
ity, they say, is the aftermath of all the drugs and their withdrawal, the long
coma, deprivation of sleep, and toxicity. It is confusing to go on thinking
as a human after entering a world that is not. Like most forms of situational
madness, it is aggravated by the coming of night. "Sundowning," it is called
in the argot of clinical medicine. Later on, the hallucinations and delusions
of this time are what will survive in his memory.

Once again the mattress upon which he has been deposited is divided
into compartments that inflate and deflate in accordance with the electrical controls at the foot of the bed. While one compartment fills, another
empties in a pattern which he is unable to solve. It seems to him capricious
and mean-spirited. At one point in the cycle, it is the entire center that col-
lapses while the head and foot rise as if to coapt, and he feels himself sliding into the abyss. In order to avoid that, he must cling all night long to the
siderail of the bed, fighting off sleep until dawn, when the dreadful contraption will at last relent. It happens during the night that a nurse will try
to pry his fingers from the siderail to which he is clinging for dear life. But
he is like a parrot in a tree, at all times hooked to a branch by one of its feet
or its beak.

Really, it would be cruel to make him let go, to place him at the mercy of such a mattress. It is a predicament made all the more desperate by the fact that he cannot utter a sound; his vocal cords, held apart so long by the tube, do not yet approximate. He cannot call out. *Help!* is a word not available to him. What does emerge from his throat is little more than a hoarse gasp that is untranslatable to the nurses on the ward. Still, his lips never stop moving. With the sheet kicked away and his body exposed he could be a schoolboy huddling under a tree in a thunderstorm telling himself stories to keep his courage up.

Then too there is his eyesight, the lack of it. Amid the frenzy of that first night in the emergency room, his glasses had been lost, never to be found again. Now everything exists in a myopic haze. Once, opening his eyes, he saw a large, undulating mass at the foot of the bed. As he watched, it distended, quivered, elongated, then thinned out until there was only a narrow bridge of protoplasm joining the two halves. Then this too vanished and where there had been one, there were now two!—a doctor and a nurse—who walked away in opposite directions. Had he witnessed a mitosis? he wondered. An episode of binary fission? Add to blindness and muteness the atrophy of his body and you have a creature that is little more than a polyp on a stalk.

Only his imagination—driven by madness—roams far and wide. In the course of a single night he travels to a medieval monastery in 13th-century Ireland, where he undergoes a harsh novitiate against his will. Minutes later he is in the delta of the river Nile, wading among the fat, yellowish serpents that are native to that region. From there, it is on to Molokai on a tall sailing ship. Father Damien himself comes out to greet him, the face of the holy man already bearing the leonine marks of his leprosy. It is no wonder that by morning he is exhausted.

He awakens to the smell of lilac and rubbing alcohol. The lilacs sit in a urine specimen jar on the sink; the rubbing alcohol is being spilled onto the small of his back, then spread by a hand with the consistency of pumice. A man speaks in an Irish brogue.

"I'm Patrick, your nurse. I'll be lookin' after ye from three o'clock to midnight every day."

"I've messed the bed. I'm sorry."

"We don't care about that here," Patrick replies. "Besides, you don't have diarrhea, it's just incontinence. When you get stronger, it will take care of itself." So that is Patrick, with his talent for forgiveness of the flesh. He is the sort of nurse who can draw the pus out of a carbuncle with his gaze alone, turn it into a jewel.

At this moment I, the authorial voice, should like nothing better than to begin using the first person pronoun, but madness, like coma, does not warrant the pronoun *I*. And so I shall continue to act as intermediary between the sick man and the outside world. We have become something like identical twin brothers, only one step closer—joined about a single heart. That accounts for my ability to convey what it was he felt in his coma and now his dreams, his hallucinations. It is only the independence of his illness that separates us. Illness causes one to go his own way unaccompanied. (Then again, the separation of our two bodies may be no more than a literary device. I can't say at this time.)

Wherever did the notion come from that flowers gladden the heart of the sick? The man has not been in his new room for more than an hour when there is delivered an ill-wrapped, ungainly parcel that, peeled down, proves to be an arrangement of seven tulips, all of the same waxen, corpselike shade of white. Immediately, the temperature of the room drops twenty degrees. They are the largest tulips of his life. A closer examination would have revealed that the long stems had been impaled on a bed of spikes and wired such that the distant hydrocephalic blossoms would respond to the least current of air. Placed on the window ledge, the evil heads are in a constant state of motion, nodding or shaking as if to vote yea or nay in the matter of his fate. At night the shadows of these flowers are magnified and thrown upon the wall—seven bald witches lunging for his thoughts.

It is the same each nightfall. He has been fed and bathed and made ready for sleep. His body, however, is not relaxed, but rigid, a corpse with its feet side by side, its eyes wide open. How does he feel? Midway between fear and despair. There is only one way to go after all: forward. Might as well put one foot before the other and march. Yet with pistol drawn and ear cocked. Oh, he would rest as he has been commanded to do, but he would not lie down. Oh no! Only squat with knees on chin. The better to stand and run.

There they are! On the wall! Sheeted by the moon, these caricatures of tulips, hunchbacked, swollen. Already, hunger stirs the mattress from its sleep. He can feel the rumbling of its bowels. Soon the dreadful peristalsis will begin. He reaches for the siderail, clutches it tightly. The night's long vigil has begun.

Ssshh! It is midnight at the Abbey of St. Ronan. Listen!

I am writing this in the scriptorium of the Abbey of St. Ronan in the hopes that one day this manuscript will be seen and the truth about my situation become known to the world. Doubtless it will be too late for my good, but there is the satisfaction of hope. It is a year ago that I was brought to this desolate monastery against my will. For surely, I have no calling to the religious life, only a handful of superstitions which do me just fine, thank you.

The truth is that I love sin. Folly, disgrace, scandal—the whole place caving in. Fiasco. If there is any sin available here, I haven't found it (that may be a lie). I was a gift to the abbot from the lord of the feudal states where my father is gamekeeper; this, in return for certain indulgences in the next world.

The Monastery of St. Ronan stands at the very edge of a cliff overlooking the Irish Sea. From the open boat, with a bitter wind tossing the ocean's white hair, it is little more than a pile of battered rocks. I am here because from childhood on, the old priest who was the private confessor of my lord taught me Greek, Latin, and the art of lettering—at all of which I have become something of a master. I spend most of my day and half the night in the scriptorium, the only place where my lack of piety is tolerated. (I make no secret of my opinion of the monastic life.) It is often said by the older monks who sit side by side with me that, had I remained in the world, I should have made a passable surgeon, so sure and steady is my hand with the stylus. It's true. Even with a badly carved pen and raw parchment, I write and illuminate more beautifully than any of the others.

My only pleasure, aside from the pride I take in my work, is the evening stroll in the cloister. At least it used to be. Until recently, when another novice, Gunther, has taken to badgering me during that hour, the only time when conversation is permitted. Gunther, damn him, is far too handsome—olive skin, black eyes and hair, a row of even white teeth. And the falsest smile in Christendom. Add to that a narrow, lewd, down-curved nose and a wide mouth. I should have guessed him to be a Spaniard, but I know he is the nephew of the abbot, a black Irishman if ever there was one. Since no one is allowed to remain alone lest he slip into solitary error (you know what I mean), we are paired off even for choir and recreation. Wouldn't you know? A hundred monks in this place and I get Gunther with his smiles and that voice all furred with malice. He is a fanatic, wants to be a soldier for Christ, and he never loses a chance to mock my underdeveloped bump of reverence.

Listen to this: at the north end of the cloister there is a kitchen garden. Bees are kept there as well. The other night as we strolled past, Gunther reached

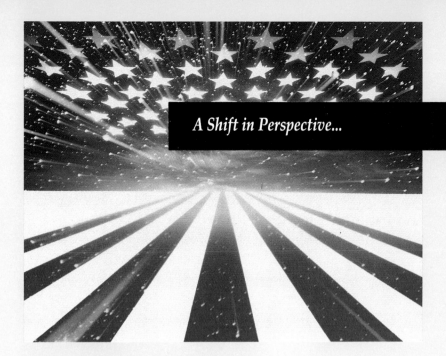

A Shift in Perspective...

Showing Our True Colors...

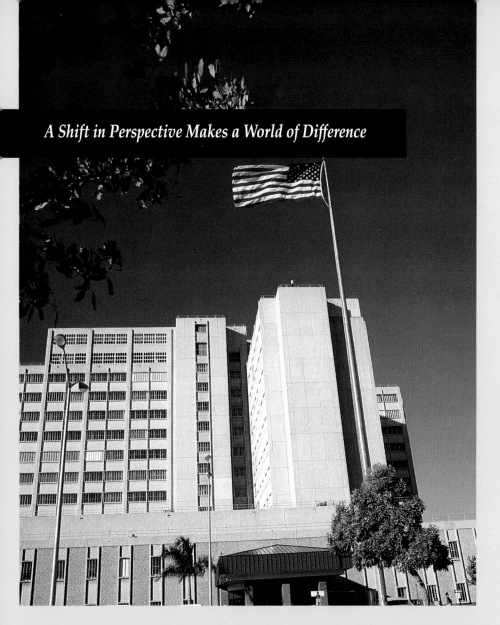

A Shift in Perspective Makes a World of Difference

Showing Our True Colors:
A Commitment to Government and Institutional Healthcare

We have a clear understanding of the needs and expectations of government and institutional healthcare providers. We recognize that value begins—but does not end—with quality products. That's why we're committed to support programs that go far beyond your expectations—continuing education programs... cooperative research...technical consultation...product information hotlines... custom packaging...and patient education. All designed to assist you in the delivery of quality healthcare. We're Marion Merrell Dow.

MARION MERRELL DOW INC.

into a hive and drew forth a fistful of bees, which he stuffed inside his habit. When I cried that he would be stung, he sang out in good cheer that he longs for it with all his heart so that he might "offer it up." You should see his little bag of whips. (Damn this pen! Must I carve them all myself?)

In spite of all that zeal, no halo swings above his head (nor is it likely to). Only the dark flame of his black and passionate hair. But about that, I shall close my mouth upon the pill of silence. I do not carry tales. Instead, I tell Gunther that he is not to feel guilty; he is not to blame for the restless blood of the Crusaders in his veins. It is obvious that he is the favorite here. Even in a monastery, beauty has its own prerogative. Never mind, my parchments will mellow for a thousand years. Who will remember Gunther and his bees?

Noon. It is hot as only Egypt is hot. Once again, I am standing in the mud of the delta. All about my legs slither—singly and in knots—venomous yellow asps, each one fat, heavy, and with a flattish penile head. I must not make even the smallest movement lest they attack. Steam rises from the Nile. Mangoes rot in the rich mud. There is nauseating smoke from fires made of camel dung. Dark red roses growing in silt. The delta of the river Nile.

Numerous barges and caiques sail downstream, the men standing idly in them. Having discharged their duties upriver, they are returning home. Free of the task of loading and unloading, they squat on the decks smoking and singing. Now and then, one will point to something on the banks—there! I follow his finger and see a group of women on their knees, dipping and pulling long strips of cloth in the water.

From four o'clock on he waits for the pigeons on the outside window ledge to awaken. Staring with myopic eyes, at last he makes out—just barely—the soft grayish mounds rising and settling as the sleeping birds are nudged by the dawn. Thank God! It is almost daylight. He could not have borne much more of this night.

Janet arrives with a large-faced clock. She places it on the window ledge next to the tulips.

"Part of the trouble," she says, "is that you don't know what time it is. And, if nothing else, the ticking will restore you to life in the morning."

"What are you talking about?"

"You're . . . ah . . . wandering? You know, sometimes you do . . ." The words of the speaker come garbled to his ears. He must reach after them, sound them out phonetically in order to make sense of them.

His three children, all fully grown, are standing at the bedside, shell-shocked. He knows that look on their faces. It is the same look as when, twenty years ago, one of them had fallen down and needed to be picked up and consoled. It is one thing to see a father in coma; it is entirely another to behold his madness.

"Stop staring at me," he orders them. He tries clearing his throat but it remains a hank of gray tatters.

"Don't you know a person gets weak from being stared at?" It touches his heart to see six eyelids lower as one in an act of filial piety. Voiceless, he delivers a sermon with his eyes, producing the words all across his face where his children might read them.

The subject is filial piety. The text: Genesis 9:20, the drunkenness of Noah.

Noah drank too much wine and while he was drunk uncovered himself inside his tent. One of his three sons, Ham, saw his father's nakedness and told his two brothers outside to come and look. Instead Shem and Japheth took a cloak, laid it on their shoulders, and entered the tent walking backward. When they reached the place where Noah lay, they let fall the cloak so as to cover their father. Only then did they turn around to look at him. Every man, he preached, should have sons like Shem and Japheth.

"You're always saying sons," says Gretchen with her beautiful, sulky eyes. "As if I weren't a girl."

"Oh, my Gretch . . ." He tries to tell her but it won't come out. He has run out of voice.

Rounds. The room is crowded with people peering down at him. A perfect stranger pulls down the sheet that covers him. What is he looking for? His toes? Yes, he cups the patient's heel in his hand, presses and releases the toenails one by one. All the while, the doctor is lecturing to the students. Another stranger bends above an antecubital fossa, sniffing, he supposes, for a vein.

"There aren't any left," he tells her. "You are too late."

"You have to start eating," says another. "It is time to become anabolic again." He waits for the doctors to leave.

Patrick enters carrying a tray.

"Lunch," he announces (he pronounces it *loonch*). "A loovely word. Makes me salivate just to say it." He pours milk over a bowl of gruel, makes as if to assist the patient, who gags audibly. "So that's it, is it? Well, if ye won't feed,

I must administer one way or t'other. Which'll it be today?"

"Here, I'll do that," says Janet. She rummages in her bag, brings forth a long wooden spoon.

"The never-fail family feeding spoon." She brandishes it. "More gall? More wormwood?" she asks gaily.

She advances the spoon toward his mouth, opening her own as if to show that love and gruel are somehow related. The man pretends to have fallen asleep. "Stop that!" he is scolded.

"Hag," he mutters.

"I am rather, aren't I?" she says brightly. "Open your mouth."

And in goes the wooden spoon.

"The food in this monastery stinks," he tells her.

"For the tenth time, you can't possibly be in a monastery, not with me here. They don't allow women." It is not sympathy in her voice, nor any hint of indulgence as though he might be a child that needed to be assuaged. No, it is more like endurance, acceptance. The man opens his eyes, recognizes her.

"Oh, it's you! What in heaven's name are you doing here?" He sleeps. When he awakens, he is alone. The sickroom is filled with the air of renunciation and obedience. His desire is to be released from it. How much easier to have yielded to the languor, gone limpsy-dewsy into death. No need then to swallow the repulsive food; no carnivore mattress; no yellowish asps. Gone too that militant novice with his mockery and his little bag of whips. It is not death that he hates; it is this borderland between, where terror and discomfort prevail. To return to life is to embark upon yearning again.

Midnight. I have just left Khartoum—a narrow escape—and am poling the caique upstream, the wooden rudder cleaving the mummy-brown water. All along the banks, in the moonlight, I see the white necks of motionless ibis questioning among the papyrus. From the shore drifts the nauseating odor of burning camel dung. Torture, bribery, flogging: that's the way things get done in Khartoum. A more miserable and unhealthy place can hardly be imagined. Dead animals rotting in the river, billions of flies and mosquitoes, the sewage of several nations floating in the current; fever, deceit, and crocodiles that can turn their heads around to look at you. And, of course, the yellowish asps with their flat penile heads. Now and then one of these will distend itself like a bladder and burst, scattering its venom, drops of which fall on the deck of the caique.

"Salaam aleikum!" I am hailed from another caique. "Baksheesh! Baksheesh!" comes the cry for alms. I dare not respond lest one of the beggars prove to be a murderous thief. So desperate are they that one or more will swim out to cling to the side of the boat, risking the asps and the crocodiles. It is well known that the Nile demands a human sacrifice for every passage upstream . . . Meanwhile, word has come that I have been reported dead and that the Royal Society is even now mounting an expedition to search for my remains, to solve the mystery of my long disappearance . . .

The doctor arrives. His name is Gordon.

"Well, where is the world traveler now?"

"Far up the Nile," says Janet. "Just passed Khartoum, I believe. A filthy place, with carcasses rotting on the riverbanks, a hundred billion flies, and crocodiles that can turn their heads and look at you."

"I didn't know crocodiles could do that."

"Only the ones in the Nile."

"How are *you* getting along?" the doctor asks her.

"This madness," she asks, "how long will it last?"

"I hope not much longer. It's the aftermath of the drugs and their withdrawal, the long period on the respirator, his own overheated imagination. And now the fever. Still, think of it this way: he has come a long way."

"If you think madness is an improvement over coma."

"This is no time to get discouraged."

"No."

"Get him to write down all his nightmares and hallucinations."

"Write them down! He can't even hold a pen."

"I mean get him to describe them to you so you can copy them down. Then you can read it all back to him later on. It's a way of splicing dream to reality. Sooner or later, he'll get the idea. I'll tell the nurses to do it too."

"I wish he would forget about that damned monastery. That's the one that bothers me the most. Actually, I rather like the Nile. Its gets downright exciting, what with all those close calls."

"Now that we've got your body under control, we'll have to work on your mind," says Patrick. Then to Janet: "What do ye suppose the hallucinations mean?"

"I know why the Abbey of St. Ronan and why Molokai."

"Tell me."

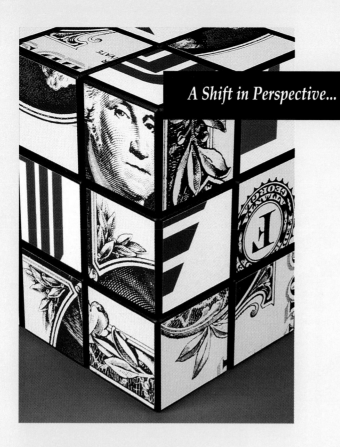

Do It Right the First Time...

"The street we live on is named St. Ronan Terrace. Once, at Christmas-time, he wrote an amusing account of the life of the ancient Celtic saint of that name. He sent the boys around to deliver a copy to each of the neighbors. Also, now and then, for all his blabbing about atheism, he goes to stay with the monks for a while; says he likes to be in the vicinity of piety. The fact is that there is a good deal of monk in him. In another century I suspect he could have ended up as one."

"And Molokai?"

"Two weeks before he got sick, he'd been on the island of Kauai giving some lectures. One of the people there had written a biography of Father Damien and had given him a copy. He was reading it the day before I sent him here in an ambulance."

"That leaves the river Nile."

"I have no idea where that one came from. He surely does get around—from Hawaii to Egypt to Ireland, back and forth across the years. As though his bed is a magic carpet."

He travels through the void at immense velocity. Where he is, there is no friction, no inertia, no resistance. It is in madness as it is in coma—no passport required. The bed is more a hippogryph than a magic carpet, one of those mythic beasts—half horse, half winged griffin—that, once mounted, can fly anywhere in the world in minutes. It is the way the sick travel far and wide without moving from the bed.

In the room, someone is whispering. "What do you think, Pat?" It is his wife asking.

"I'd estimate his horsepower at twenty-five. Might do ten miles an hour on a flat stretch. But you know . . . it all begins to fit together somehow. Saint Ronan, the scriptorium, me an Irishman, the abbot and doctor interchangeable. Those dreams and hallucinations—they do have an odd logic to them. I wouldn't be surprised if he's hanging on tight to those dreams of his for some reason. Perhaps he's looking for clues to find the road back."

And now it is the doctor once again explaining to Janet: "There are a number of causes for it." He tells her about the effect of hypoxia on the brain, the alterations in biochemistry, the breakdown of cellular protein, the interruption of synapses. She nods and shrugs. But he is wrong. It is nothing of the kind. It is imagination; it is dream. Hallucinations. What are they if not the wreckage of submerged realities?

Damien is barefoot. He lifts and gathers his cassock in one hand before stepping into the waves to greet me. The gesture is graceful, almost feminine. Then I see that the fingers of the other hand, the one he raises in greeting, are absent, only blackened stumps.

Yesterday in a corner of the marketplace, I watched as a dozen Nubian girls, each about eight or nine years old, were sold for sixty pounds apiece. The ones who don't die of diarrhea along the way will end up in the harems of the sheiks in Arabia. Three young boys, too, who will be castrated and sent to the same destination. Just as the auction ended, my presence was detected and I barely escaped with my life. Several shots were fired. And now once again I am poling up the river.

"He isn't the only one." It is a young nurse, Robin, talking to Janet. "The whole ward is hallucinating. It's weird." As if someone in a laboratory is making mirages and releasing them here as vapor.

Afternoon. Warm day in late April. The patient is dozing on and off. A woman announces that it is time to eat. By the tone of her voice she intends to see to it. Within minutes he is being fed.

"I hate gruel."

"It isn't gruel. It's cream of mushroom soup." The voice of the woman is familiar.

"Get me a pen, please, and some paper. Get me a pen! Or am I not allowed to write? Where is the abbot? Let me up! I want to see the abbot!" It is the woman's turn to cry. He seems to her ever more haggard, emaciated, yet fighting like the devil in the bed. Who would have thought he had so much strength left in him, to struggle with, to punch? She backs out of reach of his flailing arms, weeps for his chattering teeth, his hands that tremble, less at this moment from fever than from a kind of rapturous haste to get somewhere, to reach a destination. She cannot know that what he wants to get away from is his own body, stretched out, drenched in sweat and urine, smelling of decay, unshaven, with liquid stool in the sheets. Once again he gathers his fury and calls out to her.

"Get me clean parchment, a stylus, ink. The abbot has instructed me to write down my dreams."

"Just a minute," says Janet. "I have brought it all—your notebook, a pen." She helps him to get a grip on the pen, but he cannot.

"Well, you can't hold it yet. Don't be upset. It's nothing to cry about. Look, now we are both crying." She laughs. "We'll try again tomorrow."

"Visitors to see you," says a nurse. He asks his wife to leave the room. To one after another of the newcomers he struggles to tell in his tattered-cloth voice how he is being held prisoner, that he is being force-fed, that he is being treated like a child. He begs them to intercede with the abbot. From their expressions, he knows that they have been instructed to indulge him. His wife is the only one he could trust. And now even she . . .

Still later, alone and forsaken, he will peer down the sheer face of the cliff at the base of which crashes the Irish Sea. He cannot possibly climb down without a rope or a ladder.

Dusk. A nurse has finished settling him for the night.

"Sweet dreams," she sings and flicks off the light.

"Tear their heads off!" he calls after her. But she has already left and cannot hear his frantic whisper. On the wall, the tulips bow and nod. Another night at the Abbey of St. Ronan.

Really, it is quite remarkable that it ever was built in such a place and with so much devotion. The stone, quarried from the cliff itself, rough-cut, squared, then set into interlocking patterns so as to make walls and arches. These arches, mutilated by centuries of wind and rain, are held up by square columns. The stone itself is a light warm ocher that goes gray at twilight. The sun seems to endow it with all the colors of the rainbow.

I have developed a fever. In the airless dome of the scriptorium a suffo-cating heat gathers. My sweat stains the parchment which then will not hold the ink. My hand shakes so that I cannot keep the stylus steady. In addition to that, I am being watched. All because of a few harmless pranks. Tiny ve-nial sins. But around here that is grounds for being burned at the stake. The abbot, whom I had thought a fairly decent sort, turns out to be a fanatic of the worst stripe. Between him and Gunther, it is like the burning of the heretics.

By the way, I was wrong. The abbot is a Spaniard. His name is Tomas de Torquemada. A cruel name—has a ring of steel about it. However did he get himself assigned to an Irish monastery? Rumor has it that as a young monk Don Tomas was given the stigmata of the Crucifixion. Upon his ascension to the abbacy here (as the story goes), he asked Christ to conceal his wounds so as to discourage worship of his person. I'll bet! I don't know about any of that but this morning after visiting me in the infirmary, when he raised his hands in benediction, I could see bunched yellow scars on each of his palms, so maybe it is true. But I shouldn't be surprised if they were self-inflicted.

The sixth bell. Abruptly, Gunther sinks to his knees, approximating his palms beneath a bowed chin, and begins to pray. But I mean pray! His voice is strong, young, clear, his eyes dark as black olives; little drops of saliva gather at the corners of his mouth. Now and then he pauses, cocks his head as if listening, then resumes his murmur.

Look at that Gunther, will you? Easy to see that he's the favorite here. But I've got the goods on him and if it comes to that, I'll . . . If, as some say, celibacy makes one plump, he should be fat instead of lean. Well, well! Think of that! Think of that!

"Let me out of here! Let me out!"

"Now, now, stop that shouting. In a few days when your fever goes down and you no longer need the oxygen and when you start eating, you can go home. It doesn't help to shout and cry and use up your air."

"No, listen to me. Are you the one in charge here? I'm a scribe, not a monk. All this mortification of the flesh, the cincture, the fasting, it's not for me. Please let me out of here. I want to see the abbot. Take me to the abbot! I know my rights!"

At last, at last. Dawn, is it? The walls grow gray, then alabaster white. The tulips no longer cast their shadows but seem to be kneeling like monks on the window ledge, doing penance. And well they might! What is that familiar smell? For heaven's sake! Sandalwood! He remembers that they used to burn incense in the whorehouses in Troy. It smelled just like St. Peter's on Sunday. He remembers sitting there after Mass, when the priests swung the censer in the aisles, how he had had thoughts of a decidedly unholy nature. He tells that to Patrick who splits his sides laughing.

At precisely eight o'clock the abbot is standing by his bed.

"Well, how are we today?" he asks, using the papal plural. The man does not reply. "Anything we can do for you?"

"Father Abbot!" he clutches at the sleeve of a habit.

"We"—he might as well use the plural too—"are in lotus land. Help us!" The abbot takes a stethoscope and listens to the man's chest.

"Clear as a bell," he announces. The man must make the abbot understand. He must!

"Look, Gordon, Father Abbot, I think . . . I think I'm in lotus land."

"What's that? What did you say?"

"Don't go!"

"I'm not going anywhere. Tell me." He bends an ear until it is almost at the patient's lips, so as to hear.

"Lotus land," the patient says into the ear which has been presented to him. "First there's the monastery and the delta of the river Nile, then it's off to Molokai to visit Father Damien." The doctor straightens, gives the man a searching look.

"He's having nightmares," says the nurse.

"Oh! You're having bad dreams. Lotus land. The land of the lotus eaters. Now I get it!" Thank God! Thank God! What a sick person wants more than anything else is to be taken seriously.

> NOTE IN CHART: Lungs remain surprisingly clear although patient's respirations are still labored, shallow, and rapid. Fever and diarrhea persist. Worrisome. Patient states he is still in "lotus land," wherever that is. Benadryl prescribed at hour of sleep.

It takes an immense effort each time to hoist himself to the level of communication. By the time he has pulled himself up hand over hand to call for help, it is usually too late. He is terribly embarrassed by his incontinence. When it happens, he is sure he can see nostrils narrowing in judgment of the mess. He is wrong about that, of course. Dead wrong. No one cares; no one is shocked or disappointed. But tell that to a man like him who on his best days was painfully self-conscious, fastidious.

On all sides save the one facing the sea, the abbey is enclosed by a gray stone wall. It is of such a height that the top cannot be seen for the clouds that settle upon it. Often in my misery, I walk along this wall. Between the stones small ferns and tiny red geraniums are growing. I wonder what nourishes them? There is no soil, only the mortar that holds the stones in place. Perhaps it is something in the air that is absorbed through their leaves and fronds. Mosses too, of a bright emerald green, spread upon the stones, and lichen of various shades—orange, blue, grayish. From the other side of the wall, voices! Two women are speaking:

"Why doesn't he just find the gate and climb out?"

"Wouldn't you think so? It's so easy to do, but of course, he doesn't know."

The gate! So there is a gate! I don't remember having passed through it when I first came to St. Ronan. Had it been a dark night? Nor have I ever seen it since. I run along the wall searching for the gate. I run for a long distance before I must stop, panting and with my chest as though in a vise. Then I lean my cheek against the stone wall. A patch of moss—soft, cool, damp— offers itself to me. I move my head so that it is cushioned on the moss. I cannot find the gate. But I see it in my mind—a huge bronzy construction with two halves that would swing open to let a man out. The top is elaborately carved and ornamented, like a child's idea of the gates of heaven. Where is it? I must find it! I must! Now, from outside the wall, comes the wail of a woman. It is a banshee. I know it at once, waiting outside and wailing for the one who is about to die. Who could that be? The night my beloved old teacher lay dying, one of them was seen just outside the window of the room where he lay. Like all banshees, she was drawing a comb through her hair.

"Nurse! Nurse! You out there, please, I need the nurse! Help me! I'm dying!"

Awakening to the sound of bells, he wonders who has died. Best not to ask. It could be himself.

He is aboard a ship. There is the laughter of gulls, strident, harsh, the dipping of oars. What is it that he is supposed to do today? He can't remember. And then it comes to him—nothing. He is the one who is free of all human responsibilities.

Three times a day women (no, two of them are men) come in pairs and bathe him, a leg and an arm each. The torso is shared, one taking the chest, the other the back. They strip the sheets from the bed, replacing them with clean, sweet-smelling linen, pulling it tight so that there will be no wrinkles to bruise the skin. They turn him side to side in order to free the soiled bedclothes. Then he is dressed in a garment that snaps around the neck and arm, a johnny shirt. He lies between the two, yielding up to hands and cloths and lotion. He enjoys it as an infant must enjoy having its diaper changed. Each time, there is the sense of starting afresh.

Now and then it happens that even before they have finished, he soils the clean linen and they must do it all again. This they do without the least murmur, although he is in an agony of shame and self-disgust. Long after they have left the room he feels the warmth of their thighs, biceps, their breasts.

NOTE IN CHART: Patient continues to hallucinate about an Irish monastery, the Nile River, and Father Damien. Seems to have some insight into his mental situation.

Khartoum, Molokai, St. Ronan—to each of them he travels by candlelight. Everything is enhaloed by a bright ring beyond which there is the seething darkness. Precisely because it is dim and flickering, he sees more than were there wattage in the thousands.

Look there! On the Nile, a boat of cypress wood drifting; the river itself brimming; boatmen calling out and beckoning to those who would cross to the other bank; deep black pools where floats the silver lotus; light glancing off the papyrus.

Strangely, he would not trade places with anyone else even if it were offered to him. No matter how dire his condition, he wants to be himself. It is the profound egotism of the human being. Nor does he wish to waste time asking himself: who am I? Or, what am I? He knows very well both to his shame and his pride who and what he is. Nor does he even once think about God. Whatever else has changed, his atheism has remained unshaken, thank God.

Each morning a woman comes to draw his blood. She is the shape and color of an eggplant. His veins, the lack of them, are her Calvary. She has needled his arms many times to no avail.

"Must we go on in this vein?" he asks her. Unsmiling, she applies the tourniquet, shakes her head sadly. It is clear that she hates to do it.

"Your veins, they all used up. They ain't any more."

"No, they ain't," he agrees. The woman moans and he sees that her sorrow is genuine.

"Oh, go ahead," he tells her and turns to gaze out the window, willing himself to a distant land. The woman takes a large insect from a leather bag and lays it on his arm. There is a sharp sting. But by now, like Gunther, his flesh has grown contemptuous of pain.

"They all used up," the woman sings to herself. She runs her finger with obvious greed over his extensor pollicis tendon.

"No, no," he says. "That is a tendon, not a vein. Of all the tissues of my body, it is the least likely to contain what you are after."

"I knows, I knows."

"I am unclean," he says. "Whosoever toucheth my carcass shall also be unclean. Whosoever beareth away aught from my carcass must wash her clothes and bathe right away."

"Sweet Jesus!" calls the woman softly. "Keep me safe!" After half an hour of probing, she trips over a small vein. The blood runs down his arm.

"Hurry!" he tells her. "It will attract the rats."

"Oh, Lord Jesus!" she whispers. "Don't talk like that."

Just outside the door, the laughter of women. Two nurses enter the room, stand on either side of the bed. They remove his johnny shirt, strip the soiled sheets from his bed, turning him this way and that. All the while that they bathe him their laughter passes back and forth over his head. He cannot make out what they are saying. Now and then, one of them glances down, then rollicks off into another spasm of hilarity. One of them, Robin, is young, and vivacious. Is that a dark red scorn painted on her mouth? He decides yes, it is.

"Something funny about me?" he asks her. Once, in Fort Worth, Texas, he had been taken to a museum to see a collection of Cycladic art. It consisted of tiny white marble figurines, tomb ornaments used by the ancient inhabitants of the Aegean Islands. Each one a dead white color and with shoulders hunched, arms and legs thin and stumpy, eyes staring straight ahead. It seems to him, looking down at himself, that he has become one of them. A piece of statuary picked up on one of the Cyclades islands.

"You are laughing at me!" The young nurse stops her toweling, leans directly over his face. She is deadly serious now.

"Listen to me. There are not too many people here laughing at you or at anyone else. If we laugh, it is *for* you, not *at* you, so that you might hear it and be reassured. Perhaps it will be contagious and you will laugh too. If we are laughing, it is because we have to. If you worked here, I bet you'd laugh too."

Later, the nurse, Robin, and he discover that they are both from Troy, both born and raised there.

"I might have known," he tells her. "Troy, where every woman is a seeress, every man a warrior."

"Make that a whore and a drunk," she replies, "and I'm with you."

"Well, that too," he admits. They laugh together.

NOTE IN CHART: Patient expressing paranoid ideas. Thinks the staff is laughing at his body. Strongly disabused of this notion.

At 7 a.m. the maid arrives. Her name is Violet. She has the habit of humming to herself—tuneless, monotonous, held in, haunting.

"What's that you're humming?" he asks her.

The CARDIZEM family offers...

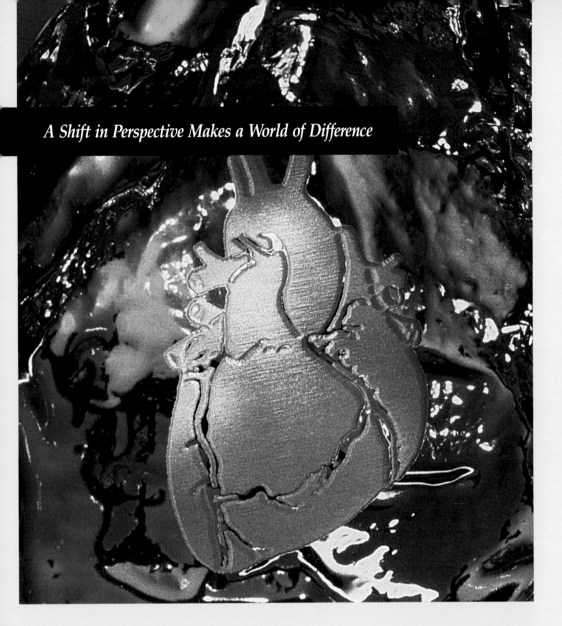

A Shift in Perspective Makes a World of Difference

A World of Support for the Cardiologist

Beyond the medical benefits of the CARDIZEM family of products, Marion Merrell
Dow provides a broad range of support and services designed to benefit the field
of Cardiology, the Cardiologist, and ultimately, the patient. Our research has opened
new areas of understanding of cardiac problems and their treatment. As pioneers
in education as well as research, we are proud to have had a positive impact on the
quality of patients' lives as well as on their cardiovascular status. From any perspective,
our heart is in the right place.

CARDIZEM ®
(diltiazem HCl) 60-, 90-, and 120-mg Tablets

CARDIZEM ® CD
(diltiazem HCl) 180-, 240-, and 300-mg Capsules

CARDIZEM Injectable
(diltiazem hydrochloride)
BOLUS/INFUSION
5 mg/mL

 MARION MERRELL DOW INC.

MISSH588/A4817

6517H2

"Hummin'? Was I hummin'? Oh nothin'. Just makin' a sound."

But each morning he reaches out to lock himself to the strange, rich noise she makes unconsciously and that has all by itself a healing quality. It confirms his suspicion that true healing is done through song and persuasion. As for his own voice, when the occasional remnant of it returns to him, he speaks in fragments, embryos of sentences, abandoning them almost at once, as though whatever it is he wants to say isn't worth the effort. Still it makes him weep out of frustration.

"What are you crying about now?"

"Tears," he croaks, "idle tears. I know not what they mean."

Two women are talking in the corridor. He, sly fox, has turned his face to the wall. He might be asleep, but he is not.

"How is he today?" That one's Janet, he thinks.

"Are you sure he isn't Irish?" The other is Robin, the Woman of Troy.

"Quite sure."

"The more you try to hide it, you know, the more it shows."

"What now?"

"Oh, he's full of the usual Trojan malarkey."

"Now what? Tell me."

"Something about Elizabeth I, that she was a boy?"

"Oh, not that old thing again. He didn't tell you that one. Say he didn't!"

"I didn't get much of it. He ran out of voice. How does it end?"

"The story goes that Elizabeth was murdered as a young girl and a look-alike boy substituted. That, he tells everyone who will listen, is why she a. looked like that; b. never married; and c. swore like a trooper."

"And he told that when he was sane? Who would listen?"

"Only the children when they were young. Here they come now. Your father's getting better—practically back to normal. Told the one about Queen Elizabeth." The way they all laugh . . .

"Eat! You must eat!" Each day and many times each day he is bidden to eat.

"Say farewell to catabolism. You must eat in order to live." But to eat without the blessing of hunger cannot be done. A dietitian comes to discuss his preferences. She is very pretty and plump. Together they will make out a menu for the next day, the correct proportions of fat, carbohydrate, and protein. He expresses his surprise that with all the advances in science there are still only those three categories. Her laughter goes all the way up the chromatic scale, like the song of a prairie warbler.

"I can live for a week on a tenpenny nail," he tells her.

"We aren't getting anywhere," she reminds him. "What would you like for dinner tonight?"

"For dinner? A glass of champagne in a crystal goblet and a single green pea." Then she takes charge.

"Fish," she says. "Chicken." The man gags at the sound of the words.

NOTE IN CHART: Patient refuses all food, states that his brain feels like a cheese—"Roquefort, ripe and falling to pieces."

Midmorning; he must have dozed off. He opens his eyes to see Gordon standing at the bedside.

"Good morning," the doctor sings with the peculiar enthusiasm of the medical profession for happy greetings.

"It is and it isn't."

"I think you are well enough to be told the facts. I'm going to try to answer your questions."

"Questions?" He tries to think what is expected of him and cannot. How can it be that a lifetime of treating the sick has not prepared him at all for the role of the patient?

"Don't you want to know what was wrong with you? Your diagnosis?"

"Oh, yes! Of course. I do. What was wrong with me? What *is* wrong with me?"

"We don't really know." The voice turns lame. The man remembers that in the medical profession one always dilutes responsibility for ignorance with the plural pronoun *we*.

"No diagnosis?" So, then. Death, had it come, would have worn a mask; it would have come anonymously.

"It's true. After all those blood smears, counts, X-rays, cultures—all the tests known to modern medicine—after all that, we are left with a diagnosis by exclusion. It couldn't have been anything else, so it had to be . . . Legionnaires' disease." He says the words importantly, as they deserve to be said.

"Legionnaires' disease? I'll take it. How did I get it?"

"All those air-conditioned hotels and planes. One of them may have been contaminated with *Legionella*. Can't tell."

"Pestiducts."

"Nice word. I'll have to remember that."

"What ward is this?"

"Infectious disease. Mostly AIDS."

"When I was 10 years old, I used to read about the Foreign Legion in the Sunday rotogravure. There were pictures of the legionnaires riding camels across the desert, close-order drilling inside the dazzling white compound at Timbuktu. I died to be one of them."

"Well, it's fifty years later, and I guess you almost did."

"That bad, was it? Must have been, from the looks of what's left of me."

"There was just nothing we did not do to get you to wake up."

"Did you try tickling?"

"As a matter of fact your boys did try tickling you. You shivered, either with agony or delight, it wasn't clear. The reactions of the body are sometimes ambiguous."

For all of that, some of the monks are rather sweetly insane. My favorite is the gardener. Yesterday at chapter he announced that under certain conditions tea made of heliotrope petals can make you invisible. He wouldn't say what conditions, and no, there is no heliotrope growing within a hundred leagues as it is a Southern flower. Once I caught him exorcising the devil from a head of cabbage! Made me split my sides. The good man avoids me ever since I told him that "paradise" comes from the Persian word for garden.

Day after day he implores his doctor to discharge him from the hospital. He yearns for home like an exile, for his study, small as a nutshell and as brown; for the house which sits at the top of a quite steep hill in the very center of the city. From the window of his study he can look down upon an archipelago of roofs, each one topped with one or two chimneys and a weather vane, and each engulfed in the foliage of large trees. Would he ever return?

"Send me home, please! I beg you on the knees of my heart, as they used to say in the old days."

"You're still having trouble breathing."

"It's this room. It's too small for my lungs. 'As pants the hart for the cold mountain stream, I gasp for wide open spaces.'"

"Oh, that is good," says the doctor. "Very good. How does it go again? As pants the heart . . . pants the heart?"

"Hart—*h-a-r-t*—you know, the deer."

"As pants the hart for the cold mountain stream. Very beautiful." He writes it in his notebook. "No. The answer is no. I will not send you home."

"But why?"

"Because you are short of breath, because you have fever, and let me be honest: you are still confused, hallucinating."

"Isn't there an old remedy for it? Apply pigeons to the soles of the feet. It draws the vapors down from the brain. There are a dozen of them on the window ledge at any given time."

"I don't want to have to worry about you, wonder whether you are okay. I need to have you here where I can feast my eyes on what's left of you. Maybe I've grown too fond of you?"

"You can visit me at home three times a day. You can sleep at the foot of my bed. I'll pull your ears, scratch your tummy. Let me go home!"

Of all the terrors that assail him during the endless nights, the carnivore mattress is prime. It is shortly before midnight. For four hours he has fended off the mattress, his right hand fused to the siderail the way a drowning man clings to a bit of flotsam, and with the malevolent tulips nodding yes, shaking their heads no. It is his tenth night on the ward. He must get out of here! Transferring his grip from rung to rung, he slithers to the foot of the bed. Pulling himself to a sitting position, he drops his feet over the side. Now he is wedged between the siderail and footboard, unable to move either back onto the bed or farther down from it. He calls out for help, but whatever voice he produces sticks to his jaws. Just as well. They would come, secure him hand and foot, deliver him up to the creature.

At last the mattress emits a deflationary sigh such that there is a bit of room. The man slips through to the floor. On the wall, the black shadows of the tulips wave in disapproval. It is the first time that he is free of the bed, standing! But the struggle has cost him dearly. He has gambled far beyond his means. He lurches to the sink and sees reflected in the mirror above it not a man, but a specter, an image of madness—mouth agape and huffing, the whites of his eyes visible all around the pupils. The nightshirt has become unstrapped from the struggle and hangs from one shoulder. "Help me!" he cries, but no sound comes.

He slides to the floor. Lying prone as in the muck of the Nile delta, he is unable to satisfy his hunger for air. Slowly, he advances one hand a fraction of an inch, then the other, into the empty darkness. His hands are the pseudopodia of an amoeba. Helplessly, he discharges from his excretory pore, feeling all of his granules blow this way and that. Suddenly the darkness produces a foot, then another. A man's feet in white sneakers. They are planted on either side of his head. In the long, shocked silence, he wonders whether the man is going to urinate on him. He himself at the moment is leaking away to nothing.

Click! And abruptly the room fills with light. From on high comes a stern, reverberant voice.

"That was a stupid and dangerous thing to do. Just look at ye, sprawled." The amoeba shudders; its granules swirl about in a kind of protozoan weeping. There is a hand at his face. "Here's your oxygen. Try to breathe more slowly. Ye don't have to pant so. I'm here, and I'll look after ye now. No, no, I shan't leave, not to worry. Look up here; watch my chest and breathe along with me." The man lying on the floor looks up toward the source of the voice. It is a man wearing a blue scrub suit. He is thickset, and has a black beard going gray. He bends over the patient. "Here, give me your hand." He places the patient's hand on his own chest, holds it there, breathes emphatically. "In. Out. In. Out. Much better." He straightens now, his feet only inches from the sick man's head. The closer foot is tapping. When he speaks again, it is in a soft, flannel brogue that is utterly devoid of reproach.

"I'm your solution," he says.

"What?"

"I'm goin' to solve ye. Trow ye into the toob, that's what."

"The toob?"

"Aye, the toob." As if to clarify, he kneels and scoops the spent, mad creature from where he lies facedown in the muck of the Nile delta, lifts him as gently and precisely as a cat taking a kitten in its mouth. "Nothin' to ye—half a pail of coal, I'd say." He hefts the patient up and down in his arms. Now they are in a small room entirely occupied by a bathtub and a wooden stool. "Fill 'er oop," says the nurse and turns on the faucet, then peels off the filthy raiment. Now and then he troubles the water with his hand, which is large, burly, and undeformed by the least elegance. The fingers are short and thick. There is a dent in the thumbnail. He lowers his patient into the warm bath, which is to the sick man like the pool of Bethesda from which the cripple emerged whole. "It's like dippin' a sheep. To get rid of the bugs and parasites.

"You're panting again. Slow it down. Breathe when I do. Yes." With soap and washcloth, he bathes the man, then scoops water with a plastic bottle and pours it over his head, again and again. Now he rubs lather into the man's scalp, massaging, rinsing. All this while, the patient lies there, neutral, incurious, breathing quietly for once. Nor does he feel the writhing of his intestines.

"Ah, just wait till I get t'rough wit' ye . . ." From where he lies in the tub he can see reflected in the Irishman's face, ruddy and shining from the humidity, the satisfaction the man draws from his work. He lifts his head, tries to look down at himself.

"What's wrong?" Patrick asks him.

"Hold me up. I want to see." He looks down at his body, lets out a groan, falls back into the supporting arm of his nurse.

"What is it?"

"My penis!" he says. The nurse casts a quick glance.

"What about it?"

"It's shrunk! Only a small button left. I knew I owed a cock to Asclepius but I didn't think it had to be my own."

"What are ye talkin' about?"

"Socrates, his last words—'I owe a cock to Asclepius.' He wanted to make sure the god was paid before he drank the hemlock." The nurse laughs.

"What's so funny?"

"Here all the time I thought ye were somethin' grand and come to find out ye're just another bloke worryin' about the size of his pecker."

At the end of a rare, sullen afternoon we have entered a natural harbor off Molokai. From the dinghy I see a small cluster of people on the beach. One, standing in front and a bit apart, wears a long black cassock and a broad-brimmed hat. Damien, I think. It is he. When he steps forward into the waves to greet me, I see the thickened tissues of his forehead and cheeks. I smell the putrefaction floating from his body; it is almost visible.

"I have been waiting for you," says the priest. "At last you've come."

Patrick leans over the man, leaning down as if to tell a secret.

"That is not true. Is it?" His voice, so gentle. And all at once, the man knows that it is not true. Only that it had seemed so.

"No," he says. "It is what I have made up." And a fresh wave of relief sweeps through him. He hadn't been to Molokai! It was just a dream.

"And all that about the river Nile? The swampy smell of the delta coating your tongue? Not true, right?"

"I have never been to Egypt."

"You have been telling stories. All right, then. We'll forget about it. No looking back. I'll miss our visits to the Abbey of St. Ronan, though. Just when they were beginning to get good. Gunther and his little bag of whips.

Really now! Behave yourself!"

At last the sick man is lifted forth from the tub, clean, calm, and sane. Rubbed dry, he is carried back to his room. The hands of the nurse have the physical kindness of big hands, the way they form themselves into a nest. Settled into it, he could laugh out loud. Perhaps he will. He thinks of how, sixty years before, his father had carried him about in his arms.

"Now how do you feel?"

"Euphoric," he tells the nurse.

"You what?"

"*Phoric.* That means being carried. The *eu* stands for contented. I am happy to be carried." And he feels the heat and the strength of the solid man infusing him, entering his veins; his breathing lightens, his brain clears into a kind of bright amazement. It seems to him that his molecules, which had been in chaotic disarray, have rearranged themselves, fallen into place. It is the true moment of cure.

As for the rest? Well, that's just medical data. The part that can be read from a computer. That doesn't make you well. Arrayed in clean linen, he lies upon the bed.

"I turned the monster off," says Patrick, tapping the mattress. "Go to sleep."

Alone and content in his solitude, he raises one arm straight up in the air. Turning his head, he sees the gesture repeated in the mirror over the sink, only more slowly, with luxuriance and absolute comfort, as if his arm were floating in a warm, viscous fluid. The struggle, whatever it had been, is far away, too far to harm him. Had it been real? he wonders, then falls asleep.

Later, before going off duty, the nurse will write in the chart: 6 p.m.: patient remains anorectic, fed oatmeal by wife despite objections. Still unable to speak audibly. Embarrassed by diarrhea. Reassured on the score once again. At midnight, patient discovered lying on the floor of his room, severely dyspneic and incontinent of stool. He was in obvious terror, stated that the electric mattress "wants to devour me," that he has barely escaped with his life. Patient reprimanded for having gotten out of bed without permission. Given tub bath with good results. Breathing more quietly; pulse regular. Long story of how he sailed from the island of Kauai to Molokai in a tall sailing vessel to visit the leper colony, how he was met at the beach by Father Damien himself. Told to stop making up stories. He agreed. Sleeping peacefully.

◆

I have been on the ward for two weeks. Every four hours a nurse appears with a handful of pills and capsules, glasses of medication. Each one as welcome as her taming was to Kate the shrew. Prednisone, erythromycin, Lasix, Benadryl, and what's that coffin-shaped tablet? Carafate, to coat your stomach. Metamucil, Pepto-Bismol, Lomotil, Bactrim. You could never mistake their names for anything else than drugs. Such a manufactured word— Pepto-Bismol—could never have been a flower. These nurses seem to speak in code. I cannot make out the meaning of what is said to me. The instructions are as if passed from mouth to mouth during a battle—*passe-paroles* that lose a portion of their meaning with each transmission.

So slowly and imperceptibly does the madness recede that when I go sane for keeps, neither I nor anyone else notices . By sometimes looking, by sometimes even not looking, I conjure the house on St. Ronan Terrace—the white paint peeling in great strips, the broken handrail, the deeply rutted driveway, the topless pine tree to the left of the front step, the lawn infested with yellow jackets, the moon coming down the staircase at night. It seems to me a far-off, bewitched place where once I lived in peaceful symbiosis with my neighbors. Now, having been evicted, I cannot find the way back. Ah! Just to think of the crystal bowl on the dining room table in which someone has floated Queen Anne's lace and the deep blue flowers of myrtle; the paintings of birds on the walls of my room—the pileated woodpecker, the turkey vulture, and the puffin. The house and everything in and around it has a glassy air of being set back out of earshot, in a time long past. I die to go there, like a boy shut up in a hated boarding school; to see home again would make me well.

Janet speaks to the doctor: "He wants to go home, says he can't get well here, says if you don't let him go, he'll sign himself out against advice." The doctor turns to me.

"What do you need that you don't have here? That we haven't given you?"

"Privacy. If I can't have that, I don't want anything."

"You do have a private room. What are you talking about?"

"I'm talking about solitude. A condition that does not include people like you coming in here whenever they feel like it and asking me what else I want."

"Aren't we touchy today?" Enter Patrick. "A regular leprechaun," he says.

"What's that got to do with it?" I have grown huffy.

"The leprechauns were all shoemakers. Shoemakers are grouchy and cross.

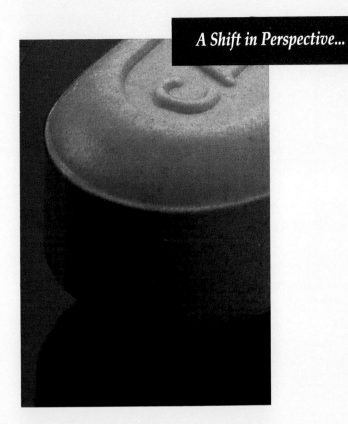

Knowing Where We Are Today...

There's no expecting civility out of them."

"And you!" I am speaking to Patrick. "The way you have of coming into a sickroom like Justice itself, then moving around in it like Mercy . . . it isn't human."

"What else," says Patrick.

"That's it."

"What you have just heard," says Janet, "is my husband expressing *undying* gratitude."

"Go home then," says Gordon. "And good riddance. I'll arrange for the ambulance. Day after tomorrow."

"Tell them no sirens. I don't want to annoy the neighbors." The doctor turns away to indicate that he is no longer addressing me.

"I think it'll be all right. Get him to bed, feed him, see that he takes his pills. There'll be the visiting nurse to check him up and put him through some exercises. If you have any questions, call me anytime." Then there is Patrick taking up my hand from the sheet, holding it, pressed between both of his.

"You come back to see us, promise?"

It is the last day of my hospitalization. In the rooms on either side of mine, young men with AIDS lie in the extravaganza of death. They have eaten very little of the provender of life, poor boys. I imagine them tossing and turning in the restless industry of exhaustion. I listen to their febrile night cries that make no sense. How well I know that in the single combat with death, the mind is at best a slender adolescent squire, standing on the sidelines.

I awaken to the sound of strange music coming from somewhere down the hall, crystalline notes made on a hollow instrument such as has never been seen before. I imagine it made of black or dark green glass and equipped with a set of clappers. It must be played with the palm or the heel of the hand. The notes are sharp and clear. *Ping. Ping. Ping.* A lovely, cheerful melody. After each note women make appreciative small screams in Spanish. I see the dark shadows around their eyes, their languor, their large pelvises and breasts. I decide against mentioning this to anyone lest my discharge be canceled.

There are visitors. A young man with a pink slap permanently imprinted on his cheek enters the room carrying a flute. He is accompanied by a woman who sets pages of music on a stand. The young man lifts the flute to his lips. It is the Meditation from *Thaïs*, a piece of music that I have always hated. The young man is earnest. There is no escape. At last, it is over.

"Do you have any requests?"

"No." For God's sake, please go away! I don't actually say this but think it very clearly so that the flutist will see the sentence written on my face. For a long moment he looks at me sadly while the slap on his cheek deepens to crimson.

Next it is a rabbi wearing a long gabardine coat, a black fedora, and side-curls. He is pale and pudgy. He hands me a sheet of literature about the Hasidic sect of Jews. I tell him I would be as at home among the cannibals. Before I can stop him, the rabbi has placed his sweaty palm on my head and blessed me.

"*Yevorechachoh*," and all that. No harm done, you say? On the contrary. Such an unwanted benediction is a form of molestation.

"Nice to meet you," the rabbi says and leaves.

In the afternoon, another musician! A woman with a violin.

"Anything you'd especially like to hear?"

"Do you know the Meditation from *Thaïs*?" When she has finished playing and left the room there is a long silence, after which Janet speaks.

"That was mean of you."

"Between the flute and the violin, give me the harmonica any day."

"Sometimes I think you are crotchety precisely because you have survived. Why else are you abusive to these well-intentioned souls?" I am silent. "No illness gives you the right to insult good people."

"I don't have to love everyone on sight, do I?"

"No, but you do have to be polite." All at once it is my own behavior that hurts. I reach out toward the door as if to call my victims back, to make amends.

"Quick! Run after them. Tell them I'm sorry. Ask them to come back for a moment. I want to say I'm sorry." I am full of shame.

"Oh, never mind, never mind. It is nothing to cry about. I'm sure they're used to it. A good thing you're going home tomorrow. You're as mean as a snake."

It is the morning of discharge. Three medical students are loitering in the corridor. First one walks by, peers in, then another. The last pokes his head through the doorway. I motion for them to come in. They have each brought a yellowed, dogeared copy of *Mortal Lessons*. Would I sign them? Yes, by all means. But the pen is turbulent in my fingers and won't hold still. The students watch my struggle in silence. I make three large X's.

"You know, before I went into the intensive care unit, I was right-handed. Now look! They've put me back together as a lefty." When they turn to leave, I collapse with relief upon the pillow. It is an hour before my discharge from the hospital. Gordon is paying a last in-house visit.

"The whole place is agog over your recovery."

"It's *your* fame that's spreading," I tell him.

"How so?"

"I'm telling everyone you brought me back from the dead. 'Get him in a good mood,' I say, 'and he'll do the same for you too.' But between you and me . . ."

"Yes?"

"Next time hold a feather to my lips. It's more reliable."

Dressed in my too-large clothes, I am waiting for the ambulance. Robin, the Woman of Troy, comes in.

"What do you like best about nursing?" I ask her.

"Waving goodbye to the patients from the window."

"But goodbye . . . it's sad."

"In a hospital, it's the other way around. Hello is sad. Hello *again* is even worse. Goodbye is just right."

MAY 5: I am lying in my own bed at home. I look around to make sure. Yes, it is true! There are my bird drawings on the wall—the turkey vultures and the pileated woodpeckers.

"How did I get here?"

"You fell asleep in the ambulance. The men carried you upstairs."

"It is my fate to remember nothing, only to be told what happened afterward."

part *four*

MAY 10: I SIT IN THE GARDEN WEARING A BROAD-BRIMMED STRAW HAT. It is unseasonably warm, they say, but even with a woolen shawl over my shoulders I'm cold. A notebook rests on my lap; I am holding a pen. With a pince-nez on a long black ribbon, I could be Chekhov at Yalta. Every few seconds I cough. A small lung abscess has developed on the left, it seems, and a new area of infiltration in the right lung. Gordon visits.

"Maybe we need to do a bronchoscopy, a lung biopsy," he says.

"Maybe I'll just cough it up instead."

Now and then I write a few words in the notebook only to cross them out a moment later. Nearby, Janet, on hands and knees, is gardening furiously. Whenever the cough turns spasmodic, the trowel in her hand assumes the same rapid tempo. I am her consultant. Do I think the yellow iris clashes with the red azalea?

"That is *their* problem," I tell her. "I never take sides in disputes among the vegetable kingdom." The pen and the notebook are present out of habit and hope: habit because they have never been out of reach for twenty years; hope because I labor under the delusion that the mere setting down of words on a page—even such words as *and* and *the*—will counteract the atrophy of disuse. The sentences I write are of no value. They are simply exercises, like the ones I must do to rebuild my quadriceps muscles. Now and again I wonder about those three weeks in the intensive care unit of which I haven't the least recollection. Coma is a black pool in which one sees only his reflection.

This afternoon a woman came to visit. We sat in the garden. For an hour she looked at me the way one looks at a river flowing by. Then, when she stood up to go, she remembered to show me the enamel of her perfect teeth in a smile.

"So good to see you coming along," she said. "Now don't you ever dare to do that to us again."

JUNE 30: It is the end of June, and still I sit in the garden pretending to write. What had been curiosity about those three weeks of coma has become an obsession. *I want to know what happened.* I close my eyes and imagine my body given over to others for them to examine in all its particularities; perfect strangers who would come to know the ins and outs of my flesh the way they know the ins and out of their shoelaces. Day after day I sit here waiting for the return of memory, but it does not come. Strange how, months later, those mad dreams will spring instantly to mind in all their lurid detail while the reality of coma remains hidden from me. Strain as I will, the membrane stays impermeable. It is no good asking others.

"You should be grateful not to know. Think of the kindness of nature in dropping a veil over all of that."

"All of what?"

"Whatever it is you say you need to know, for heaven's sakes."

"Tell me."

"Well . . . let's see . . . you were about as sick as anyone can be. You wouldn't have recognized yourself. Now just forget all about it. You're positively morbid."

But they are mistaken who would squelch the longing to know. Man's greatest pleasure is remembering. It's what makes us godlike, distinguishes us from the animals. Remembering is a way of reclaiming what was mine, what had been taken away from me. Forget it? Not likely. Janet changes the subject.

"So many yellow jackets this year! It's the lawn, gone half to clover. The bees love it." She makes a full circle around my chair holding aloft a can of insect repellent.

"If I were going to have a garden," I tell her, "it wouldn't be full of those vulgar day lilies."

"Oh? What would you have?"

"I'd plant flowers whose names mean something: sympathy, condolence, fit-of-pique."

"I'm not a bit surprised."

Come to think of it, the comatose brain is like a tree in winter, all its leaves gone, only a last year's nest remaining, high up. In May, a small scarlet bird will fly in and begin to sing rapturously. It will be spring; there will be leaves. Sooner or later he'll fly away. The tree will not remember the long sobriety of winter nor the drunken tanager.

Perhaps—I don't know—the helplessness of the sickbed, the amnesia, are more painful to a surgeon than to an internist, say, or a pediatrician. A surgeon is accustomed to authority; he is in control, he gives orders. After all,

A Shift in Perspective ...

The combining of two entities–Marion Laboratories and Merrell Dow Pharmaceuticals, each with its own distinctive personality and singular strengths–was a result of being open to new perspectives…new worlds of possibility. Marion Merrell Dow is greater than the sum of its parts, an innovative company devoted to quality… committed to research…responsible for providing a safe and healthy workplace… mindful of the environment…and respectful of our associates, suppliers, and customers. Our only unalterable perspective is the awareness that the ultimate beneficiary of all our efforts is the ultimate user of our products, the patient.

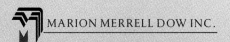

MARION MERRELL DOW INC.

are we not the warriors of medicine who, taking up spear and shield, do single combat with disease? Hack away at it root and branch? Those others, they are the statesmen who deal diplomatically with the enemy: a little more digitalis, a little less insulin. How much harder for a surgeon is the return to an infancy when he must be changed, wiped, even restrained.

July 1: In the bathroom, stepping from the shower, I turn away from the mirror, from the sight of my sad shoulder blades, my ribs. One glance is enough to make me believe that I am somebody else, yet somehow recognizable. For the first time I see *why* transvestites go to such lengths to hide what they see as their wounds. I differ from them only in that I do not want to be looked at.

Patrick visits.

"They say that you are a saint," I tell him. "Is it true?"

"Certainly."

"Good! Then I'll know at least one person in heaven when I get there."

"Afraid not. Hell has to have its saints too, as well as heaven. I'm one of those."

July 5: I have decided to read my hospital chart. All through the holiday weekend I have waited patiently to phone the record room.

"I wouldn't do that, if I were you." It is Janet making one last try.

I dial the number. Gloria answers, someone I have known for years. I request that my chart be set aside for me. "I'll be there this afternoon," I tell her.

"No problem," says Gloria. But three hours later she calls to say that my chart has been misplaced. It is nowhere to be found . . . it hadn't ever come down from the ward . . . they are turning the place upside down . . . she will phone again as soon as they find it.

"Just as well," says Janet. "Remember Lot's wife? Best not to look back."

Truth to tell, I feel some relief along with my exasperation. Perhaps I shouldn't read it after all? Four weeks later, the chart will still not have been found.

July 18: My brother Billy arrives.

"Did they finally ever figure out what you had?"

"Dutch elm disease."

"For goodness' sake, I thought only plants . . . "

"Not at all. I caught it from an infected tree. I was taking a nap under it."

He stands to leave. "I guess Jesus didn't want you for a sunbeam yet." All at once, the valves of my brother's heart swing open and I can see what flutters inside—love.

JULY 24: At ten o'clock at night the phone rings. I have been asleep for two hours. It is Gordon, my doctor.

"Just calling to see how you are."

"It's the dead of night. *Non sum qualis eram.*"

"What's that?"

"Latin for I am not what I used to be. What do you want?"

"Great doctor-patient relationship we have going here. I am just now reading one of your books. I don't usually cry but you . . ."

"Well, you made me cry plenty. It's your turn."

"Well, how are you? It's my duty to ask."

"I'm not sure. I'd have to read my chart to find out, and they can't find it." I tell him about the cough, how it keeps me awake.

"You back to writing yet?"

"No."

"Why not?"

"The synaptic spark, it's gone. All that prolonged hypoxia to the brain."

"Oh, come on! Where'd you get all that about prolonged hypoxia? You're not getting depressed, are you? Still having nightmares? Been back to the Nile delta lately?"

"I'm tired. I'm lightheaded. I can't keep my thoughts straight."

"Go back to sleep."

I lie back, thinking of Patrick. How, dipping a plastic urinal, he poured water over my head, then palmed the cake of soap and worked it into a lather.

"When I get t'rough wit' ye . . ." The Irishman's face, ruddy and shining from the humidity . . . It is months later and still my thoughts return to it as to a sacrament.

JULY 28: I am like that sultan in the Turkish fairy tale who was told by a dervish to stick his head in a pail of water. The sultan did so and when he removed it, he learned that he had aged thirty years, most of which he had spent in captivity. He learned too that he had fathered children and grandchildren.

I have the distinct sensation that every afternoon grass is growing inside my head. Three weeks and two days! People say: "In three weeks . . . " or "Three weeks ago . . ." without thinking what can happen in the space of three weeks. And two days. For some, three weeks is the gist, the core of a lifetime, on either side of which the years stretch out as if they were adjuncts to that molten, vivid three weeks. And two days.

AUGUST 1: A phone call to the record room confirms that the chart is still lost. Fine. In the absence of any record of my illness, I shall write it myself. Invent it out of whole cloth. It is what a writer can do that a doctor cannot.

Already the story begins to unfold in my mind: there is the suddenness of onset, the absence of premonitory signs or symptoms. Like John Donne, one minute I was well, and sick the next. There is the daily shrinkage of the flesh around the ever more prominent skeleton, the wild swings in temperature; there is the peripheral vascular collapse with falling blood pressure, impalpable pulse, persistent cyanosis. The X-ray shows a dense white blizzard of pneumonia throughout both lungs.

What's this! What's this! The patient is swollen with fluid from excessive hydration. How could they have done that? The liver-function tests are abnormal. Microscopic casts have appeared in the urine. And, in the corridor just outside the doorway but within earshot, are the doctors pulling at their beards, using the professional plural: "Should we add erythromycin? Steroids? What about a tracheotomy? " It is a very iliad of woes.

It shouldn't be too hard to write. Hadn't I made thousands of entries in the charts of thousands of my own patients? I know just the proper tone of voice to use—austere, pragmatic, economical. For some days, I have been jotting down snatches, not as a story, mind you, only a detail here and there as it comes back to me, small things stored in the lumber room of the mind. Sometimes though what comes back is so fierce as to abolish the time interval between the event and my recollection of it, so that it recurs in all its original fury. Then I fidget in the lawn chair and start to cough. At last I must reach for my cane and go into the house.

AUGUST 15: In the kitchen at 5 a.m. Make coffee. Cast a few grains of rice into the spoon drawer. Moments later comes the *tack-tack-tack* of tiny claws, or is it the clicking of microscopic teeth to let me know that the offering has been accepted? One must take care of one's little household gods. Also, I keep the neighbor's cats out of the house. All this I do, not in appeasement, but out of a Franciscan respect for beasts and insects. Not long ago I too was a creature on the edge of extinction, some featherless, beakless bird dependent upon the sacrifices of others. Besides, this mouse has been in the spoon drawer for months. He has many more ancestors than I. Doubtless, he feels himself more estimable than I by far.

Again and again I read over the notes I have made. And each time with increasing dissatisfaction. As a hospital record, it is adequate, I suppose. But I no longer write those. I write stories. And as a story, it lacks acceleration, crescendo, suspense and subtlety, irony, humor, the grotesque, all of the writerly stunts I have used so many times before. Most glaring is the absence of that single critical event that would raise the chronicle above the ordinary, a climax. What, I ponder, can it be that would shatter the sophistication of the hospital, the complacence of the doctors? Something, I think, supernatural, that cannot be explained in accordance with the laws of nature.

I do not know precisely when the idea occurred to me that only death and resurrection would suffice. But dying? you say. It's a bit extreme. Why tempt fate? And resurrections are tricky. Have you ever known one to come off without a hitch? Never mind. A writer will go to any lengths to captivate and entertain his readers. And I am no better than I should be. So it is decided that, after twenty-three days in the intensive care unit, I died. A nice touch, that twenty-three, like the psalm of that number: *Yea, though I walk through the valley of the shadow of death* . . .

Best, I think, to tell it with a minimum of ornamentation. No metaphors, similes, imagery. Just words of one syllable, a monochrome. That should balance whatever element of the spectacular may be inherent in the event. Only, at the instant of resurrection, there will be that silent stillness that fell upon the earth when Jesus Christ was born. Followed by a soft drumming on the roof. Had it begun to rain? Or was it the return of the heartbeat? And a lucidity that was almost unbearable filling the mind. In a moment, one's head would burst open . . .

Where to turn for a precedent? The account in the gospel of the raising of Lazarus is skimpy, to say the least. To sum up: Lazarus was a close friend of Jesus. It came to pass that Lazarus fell ill and died and was buried in his tomb. But the sisters of Lazarus, Martha and Mary, came weeping to Christ and asked why he had not saved their brother. Either Jesus was moved or else it was time for another miracle. He resurrected Lazarus, who had been dead for four days. I see the man now as Rembrandt did—sitting up in the darkness of his tomb, peeling off his cerements, a look of wonder on his pallid face.

Unlike Lazarus, I'll stay dead for only ten minutes. Considering the unusually warm weather last April, delicacy alone forbids a longer death. Besides, ten minutes is quite enough to experience whatever it is that lies on the yonder side of the grave, what the gullible call the hereafter. Already, I admit to no small pleasure at the prospect of former colleagues sheepishly probing for news of what and whom I encountered on the other side.

"How did it happen?" they ask. "What was it like?"

"It was like this: there was nothing; I was not. And then I was."

"That's all?"

"Yes, that's all."

"No, no! What was it like?"

"What was *what* like?"

"You know . . . dying, then . . . coming back?"

"Oh, that. It's like a dream in which you think, *I've already dreamt that.*"

"And the coming back part?"

"Wait a minute . . . I have to think . . . it's a cold, tingling green."

"An immersion then?"

"Not really. More like a hard slap."

"Oh."

Day by day I drift deeper into misty eccentricity. One day I may simply vanish therein. Just today Janet came into my study.

"What are you writing down there all day?"

"The chronicle of my illness."

"How is it going?"

"In a word, *marvelously.*"

"Really? Read me what you just wrote."

"At precisely that moment over the loudspeaker came the loud crowing of a rooster. After the monotonous calling out of names of doctors and phone extensions, the effect was stunning. Again and again: *Cock-a-doodle-doo!* At which, wherever in the vast hospital they were—morgue, kitchen, laundry, operating theater, emergency suite, nursery—the faithful fell to their knees, aves foaming from their lips. For it is well known that the rooster is the bird of resurrection."

"That's what you just wrote?"

"Yes. What do you think?"

"You're kidding." Silence. "Come on, say you're kidding."

To be congenial, then: "I'm kidding."

SEPTEMBER 10: The chart is written. Down to the last hallelujah. And perhaps it is not all a mere conceit, a figment of the imagination. Perhaps it is truer than had it been woven from the facts. The facts are not always where the truth lies. Ask the great historians, for whom the facts are there to be interpreted anew by each generation of scholars. Facts have a way of changing from time to time. The truth lies beneath the surface of the facts. What! you say. In coma and he can see and hear and perceive all of that? Why not? Noah saw the world most clearly during the forty days that he was shut up inside the ark, despite the utter darkness that reigned.

The more I think about it, the more real my death and resurrection become. There are whole afternoons when I have no doubt that it happened. About the next world? The truth? I don't remember a darn thing about it. Now and then, sitting in this garden, I have the faint recollection of a finger placed across my lips, shushing me. And of a voice (was it a voice?) uttering the words THOU SHALT NOT. There is a vague familiarity about it, as though I had received the same pressure on my mouth once before, long ago. So! It was as my mother said then:

"What's this groove?" I had asked her. I pointed from my nose to my lip.

"Ask your father."

"It's called the philtrum," he said. "It's where the two halves of your face join before you are born, only there is that little depression left."

"No," said Mother with all the authority of the one who had carried me in that red darkness between her hips. "It is the finger of the shushing angel, whose job it is to warn the newborn babies not to reveal the secrets of life before birth." It was the same angel on duty for resurrections.

OCTOBER 15: I have exchanged the broad-brimmed straw hat for a beret. Janet is pruning and mulching instead of planting and hoeing. I no longer cough. Every morning with my loyal cane I walk the eight blocks to the Yale library, then back home every afternoon. I have taken to pecking at the bones of an old short story, trying to prod it to its feet. There is a phone call from the hospital. It is Gloria from the records room.

"Good news!" she says. "We've found your chart. I've put it aside for you—all three volumes."

"Oh good. Well . . . yes," I tell her. "I'll come around before long." But of course I won't. It is much too late. I've already written my chart, and no mere hospital record could match it for pathos and narrative drive. Besides, I've turned my back on all of that. I'm going to spend the rest of the autumn groping my way back to my work, hoping to sprout some new green shoots from the ends of lopped branches, which so far have produced only a gray, bronchial prose. About that death and resurrection? Well, art is a means of acquiring experiences that one never had. Let's leave it at that.

DECEMBER 1: There is more than a suggestion of winter in the air, especially in the early mornings. Thinking about my Legionnaires' disease has grown tiresome. One final observation has to do with my fingernails. Only days ago, I noticed at some two-thirds of the distance between each cuticle and the tip of the finger, a fine, distinct transverse dent. Now, considering that fingernail grows at an average rate of one millimeter per week, and considering that the length of the nail proximal to the crease measures two centimeters, it cannot fail to occur to even the least suggestible that these lines were at the very nail bed itself some twenty weeks ago. That would be April, sometime during my comatose residency in the intensive care unit. What are these transverse creases if not the manifestation of some cataclysmic event that took place at that time? Rather like the geological evidence of a prehistoric earthquake or an interplanetary collision.

It takes no great leap of the imagination (mine, at least) to connect these lines with the death and resurrection that I had thought to be the product of a writer's fancy. These little marks on my fingernails give witness that for the duration of that "death," the fingernails ceased to grow and only resumed growing after the resurrection. It is further evidence, if any were needed, that life imitates art, and not the other way around. Nor has any doctor to whom I have shown these markings come up with a better hypothesis, least of all my own doctor, to whose office I raced with the electrifying evidence.

"Oh those," said Gordon, yawning behind a fist. "Beau's lines. We see them after major medical disorders—a coronary, severe pneumonia." As if familiarity could diminish the miraculous.

"So you have seen them before?" I respond. "But can you explain why they occur?"

"No, I am afraid we cannot."

"Well then," I replied and stepped out of his examining room and back into my life.

Additional Copies

To order copies of *Raising the Dead* for friends or colleagues, please write to The Grand Rounds Press, Whittle Books, 333 Main St., Knoxville, Tenn. 37902. Please include the recipient's name, mailing address, and, where applicable, primary specialty and ME number.

For a single copy, please enclose a check for $21.95, plus $1.50 for postage and handling, payable to The Grand Rounds Press. Quantities may be limited. Discounts apply to bulk orders when available. If you wish to order by phone, please call 800-284-1956.

Also available, at the same price, are copies of the previous books from The Grand Rounds Press:

The Doctor Watchers by Spencer Vibbert
The New Genetics by Leon Jaroff
Surgeon Koop by Gregg Easterbrook
Inside Medical Washington by James H. Sammons, M.D.
Medicine For Sale by Richard Currey
The Doctor Dilemma by Gerald R. Weissmann, M.D.
Taking Care of Your Own by Perri Klass, M.D.
The Logic of Health-Care Reform by Paul Starr

Please allow four weeks for delivery.
Tennessee residents must add 8¼ percent sales tax.

Advertiser's Appendix

CARDIZEM®

(diltiazem hydrochloride) Tablets

DESCRIPTION

CARDIZEM® (diltiazem hydrochloride) is a calcium ion influx inhibitor (slow channel blocker or calcium antagonist). Chemically, diltiazem hydrochloride is 1, 5-Benzothiazepin-4(5H)one, 3-(acetyloxy)-5-[2-(dimethylamino) ethyl]-2, 3-dihydro-2-(4-methoxyphenyl)-, monohydrochloride, (+) -cis-. The chemical structure is:

Diltiazem hydrochloride is a white to off-white crystalline powder with a bitter taste. It is soluble in water, methanol, and chloroform. It has a molecular weight of 450.98. Each tablet of CARDIZEM contains 30 mg, 60 mg, 90 mg, or 120 mg diltiazem hydrochloride.

Also contains: D&C Yellow #10, FD&C Yellow #6 (60 mg and 120 mg), FD&C Blue #1 (30 mg and 90 mg), hydroxypropylcellulose, hydroxypropyl methylcellulose, lactose, magnesium stearate, methylparaben, polyethylene glycol, talc, and other ingredients.

For oral administration.

CLINICAL PHARMACOLOGY

The therapeutic benefits achieved with CARDIZEM are believed to be related to its ability to inhibit the influx of calcium ions during membrane depolarization of cardiac and vascular smooth muscle.

Mechanisms of Action. Although precise mechanisms of its antianginal actions are still being delineated, CARDIZEM is believed to act in the following ways:

1. Angina Due to Coronary Artery Spasm: CARDIZEM has been shown to be a potent dilator of coronary arteries both epicardial and subendocardial. Spontaneous and ergonovine-induced coronary artery spasm are inhibited by CARDIZEM.

2. Exertional Angina: CARDIZEM has been shown to produce increases in exercise tolerance, probably due to its ability to reduce myocardial oxygen demand. This is accomplished via reductions in heart rate and systemic blood pressure at submaximal and maximal exercise work loads.

In animal models, diltiazem interferes with the slow inward (depolarizing) current in excitable tissue. It causes excitation-contraction uncoupling in various myocardial tissues without changes in the configuration of the action potential. Diltiazem produces relaxation of coronary vascular smooth muscle and dilation of both large and small coronary arteries at drug levels which cause little or no negative inotropic effect. The resultant increases in coronary blood flow (epicardial and subendocardial) occur in ischemic and nonischemic models and are accompanied by dose-dependent decreases in systemic blood pressure and decreases in peripheral resistance.

Hemodynamic and Electrophysiologic Effects. Like other calcium antagonists, diltiazem decreases sinoatrial and atrioventricular conduction in isolated tissues and has a negative inotropic effect in isolated preparations. In the intact animal, prolongation of the AH interval can be seen at higher doses.

In man, diltiazem prevents spontaneous and ergonovine-provoked coronary artery spasm. It causes a decrease in peripheral vascular resistance and a modest fall in blood pressure and, in exercise tolerance studies in patients with ischemic heart disease, reduces the heart rate-blood pressure product for any given work load. Studies to date, primarily in patients with good ventricular function, have not revealed evidence of a negative inotropic effect; cardiac output, ejection fraction, and left ventricular end diastolic pressure have not been affected. There are as yet few data on the interaction of diltiazem and beta-blockers. Resting heart rate is usually unchanged or slightly reduced by diltiazem.

Intravenous diltiazem in doses of 20 mg prolongs AH conduction time and AV node functional and effective refractory periods approximately 20%. In a study involving single oral doses of 300 mg of CARDIZEM in six normal volunteers, the average maximum PR prolongation was 14% with no instances of greater than first-degree AV block. Diltiazem-associated prolongation of the AH interval is not more pronounced in patients with first-degree heart block. In patients with sick sinus syndrome, diltiazem significantly prolongs sinus cycle length (up to 50% in some cases).

Chronic oral administration of CARDIZEM in doses of up to 240 mg/day has resulted in small increases in PR interval, but has not usually produced abnormal prolongation.

Pharmacokinetics and Metabolism. Diltiazem is absorbed from the tablet formulation to about 80% of a reference capsule and is subject to an extensive first-pass effect, giving an absolute bioavailability (compared to intravenous dosing) of about 40%. CARDIZEM undergoes extensive hepatic metabolism in which 2% to 4% of the unchanged drug appears in the urine. In vitro binding studies show CARDIZEM is 70% to 80% bound to plasma proteins. Competitive ligand binding studies have also shown CARDIZEM binding is not altered by therapeutic concentrations of digoxin, hydrochlorothiazide, phenylbutazone, propranolol, salicylic acid, or warfarin. Single oral doses of 30 to 120 mg of CARDIZEM result in detectable plasma levels within 30 to 60 minutes and peak plasma levels two to three hours after drug administration. The plasma elimination half-life following single or multiple drug administration is approximately 3.5 hours. Desacetyl diltiazem is also present in the plasma at levels of 10% to 20% of the parent drug and is 25% to 50% as potent as a coronary vasodilator as diltiazem. Therapeutic blood levels of CARDIZEM appear to be in the range of 50-200 ng/mL. There is a departure from dose-linearity when single doses above 60 mg are given; a 120-mg dose gave blood levels three times that of the 60-mg dose. There is no information about the effect of renal or hepatic impairment on excretion or metabolism of diltiazem.

INDICATIONS AND USAGE

1. Angina Pectoris Due to Coronary Artery Spasm. CARDIZEM is indicated in the treatment of angina pectoris due to coronary artery spasm. CARDIZEM has been shown effective in the treatment of spontaneous coronary artery spasm presenting as Prinzmetal's variant angina (resting angina with ST-segment elevation occurring during attacks).

2. Chronic Stable Angina (Classic Effort-Associated Angina). CARDIZEM is indicated in the management of chronic stable angina in patients who cannot tolerate therapy with beta-blockers and/or nitrates or who remain symptomatic despite adequate doses of these agents. CARDIZEM has been effective in short-term controlled trials in reducing angina frequency and increasing exercise tolerance, but confirmation of sustained effectiveness is incomplete.

There are few controlled studies of the effectiveness of the concomitant use of diltiazem and beta-blockers or of the safety of this combination in patients with impaired ventricular function or conduction abnormalities.

CONTRAINDICATIONS

CARDIZEM is contraindicated in (1) patients with sick sinus syndrome except in the presence of a functioning ventricular pacemaker, (2) patients with second- or third-degree AV block except in the presence of a functioning ventricular pacemaker, (3) patients with hypotension (less than 90 mm Hg systolic), (4) patients who have demonstrated hypersensitivity to the drug, and (5) patients with acute myocardial infarction and pulmonary congestion documented by x-ray on admission.

WARNINGS

1. Cardiac Conduction. CARDIZEM prolongs AV node refractory periods without significantly prolonging sinus node recovery time, except in patients with sick sinus syndrome. This effect may rarely result in abnormally slow heart rates (particularly in patients with sick sinus syndrome) or second- or third-degree AV block (six of 1,243 patients for 0.48%). Concomitant use of diltiazem with beta-blockers or digitalis may result in additive effects on cardiac conduction. A patient with Prinzmetal's angina developed periods of asystole (2 to 5 seconds) after a single dose of 60 mg of diltiazem.

2. Congestive Heart Failure. Although diltiazem has a negative inotropic effect in isolated animal tissue preparations, hemodynamic studies in humans with normal ventricular function have not shown a reduction in cardiac index nor consistent negative effects on contractility (dp/dt). Experience with the use of CARDIZEM alone or in combination with beta-blockers in patients with impaired ventricular function is very limited. Caution should be exercised when using the drug in such patients.

3. Hypotension. Decreases in blood pressure associated with CARDIZEM therapy may occasionally result in symptomatic hypotension.

4. Acute Hepatic Injury. In rare instances, significant elevations in enzymes such as alkaline phosphatase, LDH, SGOT, SGPT, and other phenomena consistent with acute hepatic injury have been noted. These reactions have been reversible upon discontinuation of drug therapy. The relationship to CARDIZEM is uncertain in most cases, but probable in some. (See PRECAUTIONS.)

PRECAUTIONS

General. CARDIZEM (diltiazem hydrochloride) is extensively metabolized by the liver and excreted by the kidneys and in bile. As with any drug given over prolonged periods, laboratory parameters should be monitored at regular intervals. The drug should be used with caution in patients with impaired renal or hepatic function. In subacute and chronic dog and rat studies designed to produce toxicity, high doses of diltiazem were associated with hepatic damage. In special subacute hepatic studies, oral doses of 125 mg/kg and higher in rats were associated with histological changes in the liver which were reversible when the drug was discontinued. In dogs, doses of 20 mg/kg were also associated with hepatic changes; however, these changes were reversible with continued dosing.

Dermatological events (see ADVERSE REACTIONS section) may be transient and may disappear despite continued use of CARDIZEM. However, skin eruptions progressing to erythema multiforme and/or exfoliative dermatitis have also been infrequently reported. Should a dermatologic reaction persist, the drug should be discontinued.

Drug Interaction. Due to the potential for additive effects, caution and careful titration are warranted in patients receiving CARDIZEM concomitantly with any agents known to affect cardiac contractility and/or conduction. (See WARNINGS.)

Pharmacologic studies indicate that there may be additive effects in prolonging AV conduction when using beta-blockers or digitalis concomitantly with CARDIZEM. (See WARNINGS.)

As with all drugs, care should be exercised when treating patients with multiple medications. CARDIZEM undergoes biotransformation by cytochrome P-450 mixed function oxidase. Coadministration of CARDIZEM with other agents which follow the same route of biotransformation may result in the competitive inhibition of metabolism. Dosages of similarly metabolized drugs, particularly those of low therapeutic ratio or in patients with renal and/or hepatic impairment, may require adjustment when starting or stopping concomitantly administered CARDIZEM to maintain optimum therapeutic blood levels.

Beta-blockers: Controlled and uncontrolled domestic studies suggest that concomitant use of CARDIZEM and beta-blockers or digitalis is usually well tolerated. Available data are not sufficient, however, to predict the effects of concomitant treatment, particularly in patients with left ventricular dysfunction or cardiac conduction abnormalities.

Administration of CARDIZEM (diltiazem hydrochloride) concomitantly with propranolol in five normal volunteers resulted in increased propranolol levels in all subjects and bioavailability of propranolol was increased approximately 50%. If combination therapy is initiated or withdrawn in conjunction with propranolol, an adjustment in the propranolol dose may be warranted. (See WARNINGS.)

Cimetidine: A study in six healthy volunteers has shown a significant increase in peak diltiazem plasma levels (58%) and area-under-the-curve (53%) after a 1-week course of cimetidine at 1,200 mg per day and diltiazem 60 mg per day. Ranitidine produced smaller, nonsignificant increases. The effect may be mediated by cimetidine's known inhibition of hepatic cytochrome P-450, the enzyme system probably responsible for the first-pass metabolism of diltiazem. Patients currently receiving diltiazem therapy should be carefully monitored for a change in pharmacological effect when initiating and discontinuing therapy with cimetidine. An adjustment in the diltiazem dose may be warranted.

Digitalis: Administration of CARDIZEM with digoxin in 24 healthy male subjects increased plasma digoxin concentrations approximately 20%. Another investigator found no increase in digoxin levels in 12 patients with coronary artery disease. Since there have been conflicting results regarding the effect of digoxin levels, it is recommended that digoxin levels be monitored when initiating, adjusting, and discontinuing CARDIZEM therapy to avoid possible over- or under-digitalization. (See WARNINGS.)

Anesthetics: The depression of cardiac contractility, conductivity, and automaticity as well as the vascular dilation associated with anesthetics may be potentiated by calcium channel blockers. When used concomitantly, anesthetics and calcium blockers should be titrated carefully.

CARDIZEM®
(diltiazem hydrochloride) Tablets

Carcinogenesis, Mutagenesis, Impairment of Fertility. A 24-month study in rats and a 21-month study in mice showed no evidence of carcinogenicity. There was also no mutagenic response in in vitro bacterial tests. No intrinsic effect on fertility was observed in rats.

Pregnancy. Category C. Reproduction studies have been conducted in mice, rats, and rabbits. Administration of doses ranging from five to ten times greater (on a mg/kg basis) than the daily recommended therapeutic dose has resulted in embryo and fetal lethality. These doses, in some studies, have been reported to cause skeletal abnormalities. In the perinatal/postnatal studies, there was some reduction in early individual pup weights and survival rates. There was an increased incidence of stillbirths at doses of 20 times the human dose or greater.

There are no well-controlled studies in pregnant women; therefore, use CARDIZEM in pregnant women only if the potential benefit justifies the potential risk to the fetus.

Nursing Mothers. Diltiazem is excreted in human milk. One report suggests that concentrations in breast milk may approximate serum levels. If use of CARDIZEM is deemed essential, an alternative method of infant feeding should be instituted.

Pediatric Use. Safety and effectiveness in children have not been established.

ADVERSE REACTIONS

Serious adverse reactions have been rare in studies carried out to date, but it should be recognized that patients with impaired ventricular function and cardiac conduction abnormalities have usually been excluded.

In domestic placebo-controlled angina trials, the incidence of adverse reactions reported during CARDIZEM therapy was not greater than that reported during placebo therapy.

The following represent occurrences observed in clinical studies of angina patients. In many cases, the relationship to CARDIZEM has not been established. The most common occurrences from these studies, as well as their frequency of presentation, are: edema (2.4%), headache (2.1%), nausea (1.9%), dizziness (1.5%), rash (1.3%), asthenia (1.2%). In addition, the following events were reported infrequently (less than 1%):

Cardiovascular: Angina, arrhythmia, AV block (first degree), AV block (second or third degree—see conduction warning), bradycardia, bundle branch block, congestive heart failure, ECG abnormality, flushing, hypotension, palpitations, syncope, tachycardia, ventricular extrasystoles.

Nervous System: Abnormal dreams, amnesia, depression, gait abnormality, hallucinations, insomnia, nervousness, paresthesia, personality change, somnolence, tremor.

Gastrointestinal: Anorexia, constipation, diarrhea, dysgeusia, dyspepsia, mild elevations of alkaline phosphatase, SGOT, SGPT, and LDH (see hepatic warnings), thirst, vomiting, weight increase.

Dermatological: Petechiae, photosensitivity, pruritus, urticaria.

Other: Amblyopia, CPK elevation, dry mouth, dyspnea, epistaxis, eye irritation, hyperglycemia, hyperuricemia, impotence, muscle cramps, nasal congestion, nocturia, osteoarticular pain, polyuria, sexual difficulties, tinnitus.

The following postmarketing events have been reported infrequently in patients receiving CARDIZEM: alopecia, erythema multiforme, extrapyramidal symptoms, gingival hyperplasia, hemolytic anemia, increased bleeding time, leukopenia, purpura, retinopathy, and thrombocytopenia. There have been observed cases of a generalized rash, characterized as leukocytoclastic vasculitis. In addition, events such as myocardial infarction have been observed which are not readily distinguishable from the natural history of the disease in these patients. A definitive cause and effect relationship between these events and CARDIZEM therapy cannot yet be established. Exfoliative dermatitis (proven by rechallenge) has also been reported.

OVERDOSAGE OR EXAGGERATED RESPONSE

The oral LD_{50}'s in mice and rats range from 415 to 740 mg/kg and from 560 to 810 mg/kg, respectively. The intravenous LD_{50}'s in these species were 60 and 38 mg/kg, respectively. The oral LD_{50} in dogs is considered to be in excess of 50 mg/kg, while lethality was seen in monkeys at 360 mg/kg.

The toxic dose in man is not known. Due to extensive metabolism, blood levels after a standard dose of diltiazem can vary over tenfold, limiting the usefulness of blood levels in overdose cases.

There have been 29 reports of diltiazem overdose in doses ranging from less than 1 g to 10.8 g. Sixteen of these reports involved multiple drug ingestions.

Twenty-two reports indicated patients had recovered from diltiazem overdose ranging from less than 1 g to 10.8 g. There were seven reports with a fatal outcome; although the amount of diltiazem ingested was unknown, multiple drug ingestions were confirmed in six of the seven reports.

Events observed following diltiazem overdose included bradycardia, hypotension, heart block, and cardiac failure. Most reports of overdose described some supportive medical measure and/or drug treatment. Bradycardia frequently responded favorably to atropine, as did heart block, although cardiac pacing was also frequently utilized to treat heart block. Fluids and vasopressors were used to maintain blood pressure, and in cases of cardiac failure inotropic agents were administered. In addition, some patients received treatment with ventilatory support, gastric lavage, activated charcoal, and/or intravenous calcium. Evidence of the effectiveness of intravenous calcium administration to reverse the pharmacological effects of diltiazem overdose was conflicting.

In the event of overdose or exaggerated response, appropriate supportive measures should be employed in addition to gastrointestinal decontamination. Diltiazem does not appear to be removed by peritoneal or hemodialysis. Based on the known pharmacological effects of diltiazem and/or reported clinical experiences, the following measures may be considered:

Bradycardia: Administer atropine (0.60 to 1.0 mg). If there is no response to vagal blockade, administer isoproterenol cautiously.

High-Degree: Treat as for bradycardia above. Fixed high-degree AV block should be treated with cardiac pacing.

Cardiac Failure: Administer inotropic agents (isoproterenol, dopamine, or dobutamine) and diuretics.

Hypotension: Vasopressors (eg, dopamine or levarterenol bitartrate).

Actual treatment and dosage should depend on the severity of the clinical situation and the judgment and experience of the treating physician.

DOSAGE AND ADMINISTRATION

Exertional Angina Pectoris Due to Atherosclerotic Coronary Artery Disease or Angina Pectoris at Rest Due to Coronary Artery Spasm. Dosage must be adjusted to each patient's needs. Starting with 30 mg four times daily, before meals and at bedtime, dosage should be increased gradually (given in divided doses three or four times daily) at one- to two-day intervals until optimum response is obtained. Although individual patients may respond to any dosage level, the average optimum dosage range appears to be 180 to 360 mg/day. There are no available data concerning dosage requirements in patients with impaired renal or hepatic function. If the drug must be used in such patients, titration should be carried out with particular caution.

Concomitant Use With Other Cardiovascular Agents

1. **Sublingual NTG** may be taken as required to abort acute anginal attacks during CARDIZEM (diltiazem hydrochloride) therapy.
2. **Prophylactic Nitrate Therapy**—CARDIZEM may be safely coadministered with short- and long-acting nitrates, but there have been no controlled studies to evaluate the antianginal effectiveness of this combination.
3. **Beta-blockers.** (See WARNINGS and PRECAUTIONS.)

HOW SUPPLIED

CARDIZEM 30-mg tablets are supplied in bottles of 100 (NDC 0088-1771-47) and 500 (NDC 0088-1771-55), and in Unit Dose Identification Paks of 100 (NDC 0088-1771-49). Each green tablet is engraved with MARION on one side and 1771 engraved on the other.

CARDIZEM 60-mg scored tablets are supplied in bottles of 90 (NDC 0088-1772-42), 100 (NDC 0088-1772-47), 500 (NDC 0088-1772-55), and in Unit Dose Identification Paks of 100 (NDC 0088-1772-49). Each yellow tablet is engraved with MARION on one side and 1772 engraved on the other.

CARDIZEM 90-mg scored tablets are supplied in bottles of 90 (NDC 0088-1791-42), and 100 (NDC 0088-1791-47), and in Unit Dose Identification Paks of 100 (NDC 0088-1791-49). Each green oblong tablet is engraved with CARDIZEM on one side and 90 mg engraved on the other.

CARDIZEM 120-mg scored tablets are supplied in bottles of 90 (NDC 0088-1792-42), and 100 (NDC 0088-1792-47), and in Unit Dose Identification Paks of 100 (NDC 0088-1792-49). Each yellow oblong tablet is engraved with CARDIZEM on one side and 120 mg engraved on the other.

Store at controlled room temperature 59-86°F (15-30°C).

Issued 1/91

MARION MERRELL DOW INC.
PRESCRIPTION PRODUCTS DIVISION
KANSAS CITY, MO 64114

CARDIZEM® CD
(diltiazem HCl)
Capsules

DESCRIPTION
CARDIZEM® (diltiazem hydrochloride) is a calcium ion influx inhibitor (slow channel blocker or calcium antagonist). Chemically, diltiazem hydrochloride is 1,5-Benzothiazepin-4(5H)one,3-(acetyloxy)-5-[2-(dimethylamino)ethyl]-2,3-dihydro-2-(4-methoxyphenyl)-, monohydrochloride,(+)-cis-. The chemical structure is:

Diltiazem hydrochloride is a white to off-white crystalline powder with a bitter taste. It is soluble in water, methanol and chloroform. It has a molecular weight of 450.98. CARDIZEM CD is formulated as a once-a-day extended release capsule containing either 120 mg, 180 mg, 240 mg, or 300 mg diltiazem hydrochloride.

Also contains: black iron oxide, ethylcellulose, FD&C Blue #1, fumaric acid, gelatin-NF, sucrose, starch, talc, titanium dioxide, white wax, and other ingredients. For oral administration.

CLINICAL PHARMACOLOGY
The therapeutic effects of CARDIZEM CD are believed to be related to its ability to inhibit the influx of calcium ions during membrane depolarization of cardiac and vascular smooth muscle.

Mechanisms of Action
Hypertension. CARDIZEM CD produces its antihypertensive effect primarily by relaxation of vascular smooth muscle and the resultant decrease in peripheral vascular resistance. The magnitude of blood pressure reduction is related to the degree of hypertension; thus hypertensive individuals experience an antihypertensive effect, whereas there is only a modest fall in blood pressure in normotensives.

Angina. CARDIZEM CD has been shown to produce increases in exercise tolerance, probably due to its ability to reduce myocardial oxygen demand. This is accomplished via reductions in heart rate and systemic blood pressure at submaximal and maximal work loads. Diltiazem has been shown to be a potent dilator of coronary arteries, both epicardial and subendocardial. Spontaneous and ergonovine-induced coronary artery spasm are inhibited by diltiazem.

In animal models, diltiazem interferes with the slow inward (depolarizing) current in excitable tissue. It causes excitation-contraction uncoupling in various myocardial tissues without changes in the configuration of the action potential. Diltiazem produces relaxation of coronary vascular smooth muscle and dilation of both large and small coronary arteries at drug levels which cause little or no negative inotropic effect. The resultant increases in coronary blood flow (epicardial and subendocardial) occur in ischemic and nonischemic models and are accompanied by dose-dependent decreases in systemic blood pressure and decreases in peripheral resistance.

Hemodynamic and Electrophysiologic Effects
Like other calcium channel antagonists, diltiazem decreases sinoatrial and atrioventricular conduction in isolated tissues and has a negative inotropic effect in isolated preparations. In the intact animal, prolongation of the AH interval can be seen at higher doses.

In man, diltiazem prevents spontaneous and ergonovine-provoked coronary artery spasm. It causes a decrease in peripheral vascular resistance and a modest fall in blood pressure in normotensive individuals and, in exercise tolerance studies in patients with ischemic heart disease, reduces the heart rate-blood pressure product for any given work load. Studies to date, primarily in patients with good ventricular function, have not revealed evidence of a negative inotropic effect; cardiac output, ejection fraction, and left ventricular end diastolic pressure have not been affected. Such data have no predictive value with respect to effects in patients with poor ventricular function, and increased heart failure has been reported in patients with preexisting impairment of ventricular function. There are as yet few data on the interaction of diltiazem and beta-blockers in patients with poor ventricular function. Resting heart rate is usually slightly reduced by diltiazem.

In hypertensive patients, CARDIZEM CD produces antihypertensive effects both in the supine and standing positions. In a double-blind, parallel, dose-response study utilizing doses ranging from 90 to 540 mg once daily, CARDIZEM CD lowered supine diastolic blood pressure in an apparent linear manner over the entire dose range studied. The changes in diastolic blood pressure, measured at trough, for placebo, 90 mg, 180 mg, 360 mg, and 540 mg were -2.9, -4.5, -6.1, -9.5, and -10.5 mm Hg, respectively. Postural hypotension is infrequently noted upon suddenly assuming an upright position. No reflex tachycardia is associated with the chronic antihypertensive effects. CARDIZEM CD decreases vascular resistance, increases cardiac output (by increasing stroke volume), and produces a slight decrease or no change in heart rate. During dynamic exercise, increases in diastolic pressure are inhibited while maximum achievable systolic pressure is usually reduced. Chronic therapy with CARDIZEM CD produces no change or an increase in plasma catecholamines. No increased activity of the renin-angiotensin-aldosterone axis has been observed. CARDIZEM CD reduces the renal and peripheral effects of angiotensin II. Hypertensive animal models respond to diltiazem with reductions in blood pressure and increased urinary output and natriuresis without a change in urinary sodium/potassium ratio.

In a double-blind, parallel dose response study of doses from 60 mg to 480 mg once daily, CARDIZEM CD increased time to termination of exercise in a linear manner over the entire dose range studied. The improvement in time to termination of exercise utilizing a Bruce exercise protocol, measured at trough, for placebo, 60 mg, 120 mg, 240 mg, 360 mg, and 480 mg was 29, 40, 56, 51, 69 and 68 seconds, respectively. As doses of CARDIZEM CD were increased, overall angina frequency was decreased. CARDIZEM CD, 180 mg once daily, or placebo was administered in a double-blind study to patients receiving concomitant treatment with long-acting nitrates and/or beta-blockers. A significant increase in time to termination of exercise and a significant decrease in overall angina frequency was observed. In this trial the overall frequency of adverse events in the CARDIZEM CD treatment group was the same as the placebo group.

Intravenous diltiazem in doses of 20 mg prolongs AH conduction time and AV node functional and effective refractory periods by approximately 20%. In a study involving single oral doses of 300 mg of CARDIZEM in six normal volunteers, the average maximum PR prolongation was 14% with no instances of greater than first-degree AV block. Diltiazem-associated prolongation of the AH interval is not more pronounced in patients with first-degree heart block. In patients with sick sinus syndrome, diltiazem significantly prolongs sinus cycle length (up to 50% in some cases). Chronic oral administration of CARDIZEM to patients in doses of up to 540 mg/day has resulted in small increases in PR interval, and on occasion produces abnormal prolongation. (See WARNINGS.)

Pharmacokinetics and Metabolism
Diltiazem is well absorbed from the gastrointestinal tract and is subject to an extensive first-pass effect, giving an absolute bioavailability (compared to intravenous administration) of about 40%. CARDIZEM undergoes extensive metabolism in which only 2% to 4% of the unchanged drug appears in the urine. Drugs which induce or inhibit hepatic microsomal enzymes may alter diltiazem disposition.

Total radioactivity measurement following short IV administration in healthy volunteers suggests the presence of other unidentified metabolites which attain higher concentrations than those of diltiazem and are more slowly eliminated; half-life of total radioactivity is about 20 hours compared to 2 to 5 hours for diltiazem.

In vitro binding studies show CARDIZEM is 70% to 80% bound to plasma proteins. Competitive in vitro ligand binding studies have also shown CARDIZEM binding is not altered by therapeutic concentrations of digoxin, hydrochlorothiazide, phenylbutazone, propranolol, salicylic acid, or warfarin. The plasma elimination half-life following single or multiple drug administration is approximately 3.0 to 4.5 hours. Desacetyl diltiazem is also present in the plasma at levels of 10% to 20% of the parent drug and is 25% to 50% as potent as a coronary vasodilator as diltiazem. Minimum therapeutic plasma diltiazem concentrations appear to be in the range of 50 to 200 ng/mL. There is a departure from linearity when dose strengths are increased; the half-life is slightly increased with dose. A study that compared patients with normal hepatic function to patients with cirrhosis found an increase in half-life and a 69% increase in bioavailability in the hepatically impaired patients. A single study in patients with severely impaired renal function showed no difference in the pharmacokinetic profile of diltiazem compared to patients with normal renal function.

CARDIZEM CD Capsules
When compared to a regimen of CARDIZEM tablets at steady-state, more than 95% of drug is absorbed from the CARDIZEM CD formulation. A single 360-mg dose of the capsule results in detectable plasma levels within 2 hours and peak plasma levels between 10 and 14 hours; absorption occurs throughout the dosing interval. When CARDIZEM CD was coadministered with a high fat content breakfast, the extent of diltiazem absorption was not affected. Dose-dumping does not occur. The apparent elimination half-life after single or multiple dosing is 5 to 8 hours. A departure from linearity similar to that seen with CARDIZEM tablets and CARDIZEM SR capsules is observed. As the dose of CARDIZEM CD capsules is increased from a daily dose of 120 mg to 240 mg, there is an increase in the area-under-the-curve of 2.7 times. When the dose is increased from 240 mg to 360 mg there is an increase in the area-under-the-curve of 1.6 times.

INDICATIONS AND USAGE
CARDIZEM CD is indicated for the treatment of hypertension. It may be used alone or in combination with other antihypertensive medications.

CARDIZEM CD is indicated for the management of chronic stable angina and angina due to coronary artery spasm.

CONTRAINDICATIONS
CARDIZEM is contraindicated in (1) patients with sick sinus syndrome except in the presence of a functioning ventricular pacemaker, (2) patients with second- or third-degree AV block except in the presence of a functioning ventricular pacemaker, (3) patients with hypotension (less than 90 mm Hg systolic), (4) patients who have demonstrated hypersensitivity to the drug, and (5) patients with acute myocardial infarction and pulmonary congestion documented by x-ray on admission.

WARNINGS
1. **Cardiac Conduction**. CARDIZEM prolongs AV node refractory periods without significantly prolonging sinus node recovery time, except in patients with sick sinus syndrome. This effect may rarely result in abnormally slow heart rates (particularly in patients with sick sinus syndrome) or second- or third-degree AV block (13 of 3,290 patients or 0.40%). Concomitant use of diltiazem with beta-blockers or digitalis may result in additive effects on cardiac conduction. A patient with Prinzmetal's angina developed periods of asystole (2 to 5 seconds) after a single dose of 60 mg of diltiazem.

2. **Congestive Heart Failure**. Although diltiazem has a negative inotropic effect in isolated animal tissue preparations, hemodynamic studies in humans with normal ventricular function have not shown a reduction in cardiac index nor consistent negative effects on contractility (dp/dt). An acute study of diltiazem in patients with impaired ventricular function (ejection fraction 24% ± 6%) showed improvement in indices of ventricular function without significant decrease in contractile function (dp/dt). Worsening of congestive heart failure has been reported in patients with preexisting impairment of ventricular function. Experience with the use of CARDIZEM (diltiazem hydrochloride) in combination with beta-blockers in patients with impaired ventricular function is limited. Caution should be exercised when using this combination.

3. **Hypotension**. Decreases in blood pressure associated with CARDIZEM therapy may occasionally result in symptomatic hypotension.

4. **Acute Hepatic Injury**. Mild elevations of transaminases with and without concomitant elevation in alkaline phosphatase and bilirubin have been observed in clinical studies. Such elevations were usually transient and frequently resolved even with continued diltiazem treatment. In rare instances, significant elevations in enzymes such as alkaline phosphatase, LDH, SGOT, SGPT, and other phenomena consistent with acute hepatic injury have been noted. These reactions tended to occur early after therapy initiation (1 to 8 weeks) and have been reversible upon discontinuation of drug therapy. The relationship to CARDIZEM is uncertain in some cases, but probable in some. (See PRECAUTIONS.)

PRECAUTIONS
General
CARDIZEM (diltiazem hydrochloride) is extensively metabolized by the liver and excreted by the kidneys and in bile. As with any drug given over prolonged periods, laboratory parameters of renal and hepatic function should be monitored at regular intervals. The drug should be used with caution in patients with impaired renal or hepatic function. In subacute and chronic dog and rat studies designed to produce toxicity, high doses of diltiazem were associated with hepatic damage. In special subacute hepatic studies, oral doses of 125 mg/kg and higher in rats were associated with histological changes in the liver which were reversible when the drug was discontinued. In dogs, doses of 20 mg/kg were also associated with hepatic changes; however, these changes were reversible with continued dosing.

Dermatological events (see ADVERSE REACTIONS section) may be transient and may disappear despite continued use of CARDIZEM. However, skin eruptions progressing to erythema multiforme and/or exfoliative dermatitis have also been infrequently reported. Should a dermatologic reaction persist, the drug should be discontinued.

Drug Interactions
Due to the potential for additive effects, caution and careful titration are warranted in patients receiving CARDIZEM concomitantly with other agents known to affect cardiac contractility and/or conduction. (See WARNINGS.) Pharmacologic studies indicate that there may be additive effects in prolonging AV conduction when using beta-blockers or digitalis concomitantly with CARDIZEM. (See WARNINGS.)

As with all drugs, care should be exercised when treating patients with multiple medications. CARDIZEM undergoes biotransformation by cytochrome P-450 mixed function oxidase. Coadministration of CARDIZEM with other agents which follow the same route of biotransformation may result in the competitive inhibition of metabolism. Dosages of similarly metabolized drugs such as cyclosporin, particularly those of low therapeutic ratio or in patients with renal and/or hepatic impairment, may require adjustment when starting or stopping concomitantly administered CARDIZEM to maintain optimum therapeutic blood levels.

Beta-blockers. Controlled and uncontrolled domestic studies suggest that concomitant use of CARDIZEM and beta-blockers is usually well tolerated, but available data are not sufficient to predict the effects of concomitant treatment in patients with left ventricular dysfunction or cardiac conduction abnormalities.

Administration of CARDIZEM (diltiazem hydrochloride) concomitantly with propranolol in five normal volunteers resulted in increased propranolol levels in all subjects and bioavailability of propranolol was increased approximately 50%. In vitro, propranolol appears to be displaced from its binding sites by diltiazem. If combination therapy is initiated or withdrawn in conjunction with propranolol, an adjustment in the propranolol dose may be warranted. (See WARNINGS.)

Cimetidine. A study in six healthy volunteers has shown a significant increase in peak diltiazem plasma levels (58%) and area-under-the-curve (53%) after a 1-week course of cimetidine at 1200 mg per day and a single dose of diltiazem 60 mg. Ranitidine produced smaller, nonsignificant increases. The effect may be mediated by cimetidine's known inhibition of hepatic cytochrome P-450, the enzyme system responsible for the first-pass metabolism of diltiazem. Patients currently receiving diltiazem therapy should be carefully monitored for a change in pharmacological effect when initiating and discontinuing therapy with cimetidine. An adjustment in the diltiazem dose may be warranted.

Digitalis. Administration of CARDIZEM with digoxin in 24 healthy male subjects increased plasma digoxin concentrations approximately 20%. Another investigator found no increase in digoxin levels in 12 patients with coronary artery disease. Since there have been conflicting results regarding the effect of digoxin levels, it is recommended that digoxin levels be monitored when initiating, adjusting, and discontinuing CARDIZEM therapy to avoid possible over- or under-digitalization. (See WARNINGS.)

Anesthetics. The depression of cardiac contractility, conductivity, and automaticity as well as the vascular dilation associated with anesthetics may be potentiated by calcium channel blockers. When used concomitantly, anesthetics and calcium blockers should be titrated carefully.

Carcinogenesis, Mutagenesis, Impairment of Fertility
A 24-month study in rats at oral dosage levels of up to 100 mg/kg/day and a 21-month study in mice at oral dosage levels of up to 30 mg/kg/day showed no evidence of carcinogenicity. There was also no mutagenic response in vitro or in vivo in mammalian cell assays or in vitro in bacteria. No evidence of impaired fertility was observed in a study performed in male and female rats at oral dosages of up to 100 mg/kg/day.

Pregnancy
Category C. Reproduction studies have been conducted in mice, rats, and rabbits. Administration of doses ranging from five to ten times greater (on a mg/kg basis) than the daily recommended therapeutic dose has resulted in embryo and fetal lethality. These doses, in some studies, have been reported to cause skeletal abnormalities. In the perinatal/postnatal studies, there was an increased incidence of stillbirths at doses of 20 times the human dose or greater.

There are no well-controlled studies in pregnant women; therefore, use CARDIZEM in pregnant women only if the potential benefit justifies the potential risk to the fetus.

Nursing Mothers. Diltiazem is excreted in human milk. One report suggests that concentrations in breast milk may approximate serum levels. If use of CARDIZEM is deemed essential, an alternative method of infant feeding should be instituted.

Pediatric Use. Safety and effectiveness in children have not been established.

ADVERSE REACTIONS
Serious adverse reactions have been rare in studies carried out to date, but it should be recognized that patients with impaired ventricular function and cardiac conduction abnormalities have usually been excluded from these studies.

The following table presents the most common adverse reactions reported in placebo-controlled angina and hypertension trials in patients receiving CARDIZEM CD up to 360 mg with rates in placebo patients shown for comparison.

CARDIZEM CD Capsule Placebo-Controlled Angina and Hypertension Trials Combined		
Adverse Reaction	Cardizem CD N=607	Placebo N=301
Headache	5.4%	5.0%
Dizziness	3.0%	3.0%
Bradycardia	3.3%	1.3%
AV Block First Degree	3.3%	0.0%
Edema	2.6%	1.3%
ECG Abnormality	1.6%	2.3%
Asthenia	1.8%	1.7%

CARDIZEM® CD
(diltiazem HCl)

In clinical trials of CARDIZEM CD Capsules, CARDIZEM Tablets, and CARDIZEM SR Capsules involving over 3200 patients, the most common events (ie, greater than 1%) were edema (4.6%), headache (4.6%), dizziness (3.5%), asthenia (2.6%), first-degree AV block (2.4%), bradycardia (1.7%), flushing (1.4%), nausea (1.4%), and rash (1.2%). In addition, the following events were reported infrequently (less than 1%) in angina or hypertension trials:

Cardiovascular: Angina, arrhythmia, AV block (second- or third-degree), bundle branch block, congestive heart failure, ECG abnormalities, hypotension, palpitations, syncope, tachycardia, ventricular extrasystoles

Nervous System: Abnormal dreams, amnesia, depression, gait abnormality, hallucinations, insomnia, nervousness, paresthesia, personality change, somnolence, tinnitus, tremor

Gastrointestinal: Anorexia, constipation, diarrhea, dry mouth, dysgeusia, dyspepsia, mild elevations of SGOT, SGPT, LDH, and alkaline phosphatase (see hepatic warnings), thirst, vomiting, weight increase

Dermatological: Petechiae, photosensitivity, pruritus, urticaria

Other: Amblyopia, CPK increase, dyspnea, epistaxis, eye irritation, hyperglycemia, hyperuricemia, impotence, muscle cramps, nasal congestion, nocturia, osteoarticular pain, polyuria, sexual difficulties

The following postmarketing events have been reported infrequently in patients receiving CARDIZEM: alopecia, erythema multiforme, exfoliative dermatitis, extrapyramidal symptoms, gingival hyperplasia, hemolytic anemia, increased bleeding time, leukopenia, purpura, retinopathy, and thrombocytopenia. In addition, events such as myocardial infarction have been observed which are not readily distinguishable from the natural history of the disease in these patients. A number of well-documented cases of generalized rash, characterized as leukocytoclastic vasculitis, have been reported. However, a definitive cause and effect relationship between these events and CARDIZEM therapy is yet to be established.

OVERDOSAGE

The oral LD_{50}'s in mice and rats range from 415 to 740 mg/kg and from 560 to 810 mg/kg, respectively. The intravenous LD_{50}'s in these species were 60 and 38 mg/kg, respectively. The oral LD_{50} in dogs is considered to be in excess of 50 mg/kg, while lethality was seen in monkeys at 360 mg/kg.

The toxic dose in man is not known. Due to extensive metabolism, blood levels after a standard dose of diltiazem can vary over tenfold, limiting the usefulness of blood levels in overdose cases.

There have been 29 reports of diltiazem overdose in doses ranging from less than 1 gm to 10.8 gm. Sixteen of these reports involved multiple drug ingestions.

Twenty-two reports indicated patients had recovered from diltiazem overdose ranging from less than 1 gm to 10.8 gm. There were seven reports with a fatal outcome; although the amount of diltiazem ingested was unknown, multiple drug ingestions were confirmed in six of the seven reports.

Events observed following diltiazem overdose included bradycardia, hypotension, heart block, and cardiac failure. Most reports of overdose described some supportive medical measure and/or drug treatment. Bradycardia frequently responded favorably to atropine as did heart block, although cardiac pacing was also frequently utilized to treat heart block. Fluids and vasopressors were used to maintain blood pressure, and in cases of cardiac failure, inotropic agents were administered. In addition, some patients received treatment with ventilatory support, gastric lavage, activated charcoal, and/or intravenous calcium. Evidence of the effectiveness of intravenous calcium administration to reverse the pharmacological effects of diltiazem overdose was conflicting.

In the event of overdose or exaggerated response, appropriate supportive measures should be employed in addition to gastrointestinal decontamination. Diltiazem does not appear to be removed by peritoneal or hemodialysis. Based on the known pharmacological effects of diltiazem and/or reported clinical experiences, the following measures may be considered:

Bradycardia: Administer atropine (0.60 to 1.0 mg). If there is no response to vagal blockade, administer isoproterenol cautiously

High-degree AV Block: Treat as for bradycardia above. Fixed high-degree AV block should be treated with cardiac pacing

Cardiac Failure: Administer inotropic agents (isoproterenol, dopamine, or dobutamine) and diuretics

Hypotension: Vasopressors (eg, dopamine or levarterenol bitartrate)

Actual treatment and dosage should depend on the severity of the clinical situation and the judgment and experience of the treating physician.

DOSAGE AND ADMINISTRATION

Patients controlled on diltiazem alone or in combination with other medications may be safely switched to CARDIZEM CD capsules at the nearest equivalent total daily dose. Subsequent titration to higher or lower doses may be necessary and should be initiated as clinically warranted. There is limited general clinical experience with doses above 360 mg, but doses to 540 mg have been studied in clinical trials. The incidence of side effects increases as the dose increases with first-degree AV block, dizziness and sinus bradycardia bearing the strongest relationship to dose.

Hypertension. Dosage needs to be adjusted by titration to individual patient needs. When used as monotherapy, reasonable starting doses are 180 to 240 mg once daily, although some patients may respond to lower doses. Maximum antihypertensive effect is usually observed by 14 days of chronic therapy; therefore, dosage adjustments should be scheduled accordingly. The usual dosage range studied in clinical trials was 240 to 360 mg once daily. Individual patients may respond to higher doses of up to 480 mg once daily.

Angina. Dosages for the treatment of angina should be adjusted to each patient's needs, starting with a dose of 120 or 180 mg once daily. Individual patients may respond to higher doses of up to 480 mg once daily. When necessary, titration may be carried out over a 7 to 14 day period.

Concomitant Use With Other Cardiovascular Agents.

1. **Sublingual NTG** may be taken as required to abort acute anginal attacks during CARDIZEM CD (diltiazem hydrochloride) therapy.
2. **Prophylactic Nitrate Therapy**—CARDIZEM CD may be safely coadministered with short- and long-acting nitrates.
3. **Beta-blockers**. (See WARNINGS and PRECAUTIONS.)
4. **Antihypertensives**—CARDIZEM CD has an additive antihypertensive effect when used with other antihypertensive agents. Therefore, the dosage of CARDIZEM CD or the concomitant antihypertensives may need to be adjusted when adding one to the other.

HOW SUPPLIED

CARDIZEM® CD (diltiazem hydrochloride) Capsules			
Strength	Quantity	NDC Number	Description
120 mg	30 btl 90 btl 100 UDIP®	0088-1795-30 0088-1795-42 0088-1795-49	Light turquoise blue/light turquoise blue capsule imprinted with the Marion Merrell Dow Inc. logo on one end and CARDIZEM CD and 120 mg on the other.
180 mg	30 btl 90 btl 100 UDIP®	0088-1796-30 0088-1796-42 0088-1796-49	Light turquoise blue/blue capsule imprinted with the Marion Merrell Dow Inc. logo on one end and CARDIZEM CD and 180 mg on the other.
240 mg	30 btl 90 btl 100 UDIP®	0088-1797-30 0088-1797-42 0088-1797-49	Blue/blue capsule imprinted with the Marion Merrell Dow Inc. logo on one end and CARDIZEM CD and 240 mg on the other.
300 mg	30 btl 90 btl 100 UDIP®	0088-1798-30 0088-1798-42 0088-1798-49	Light gray/blue capsule imprinted with the Marion Merrell Dow Inc. logo on one end and CARDIZEM CD and 300 mg on the other.

Storage Conditions: Store at controlled room temperature 59-86° F (15-30°C). Avoid excessive humidity.

Prescribing Information as of October 1992 (2)

Marion Merrell Dow Inc.
Kansas City, MO 64114

ccdp1092(2)e

CARDIZEM® Injectable
(diltiazem hydrochloride)

DESCRIPTION

CARDIZEM® (diltiazem hydrochloride) is a calcium ion influx inhibitor (slow channel blocker or calcium channel antagonist). Chemically, diltiazem hydrochloride is 1,5-benzothiazepin-4(5H)one,3-(acetyloxy)-5-[2-(dimethylamino)ethyl]-2,3-dihydro-2-(4-methoxyphenyl)-, monohydrochloride,(+)-cis-. The chemical structure is:

Diltiazem hydrochloride is a white to off-white crystalline powder with a bitter taste. It is soluble in water, methanol, and chloroform. It has a molecular weight of 450.98.

CARDIZEM Injectable (diltiazem hydrochloride) is a clear, colorless, sterile, nonpyrogenic solution. It has a pH range of 3.7 to 4.1.

CARDIZEM Injectable is for direct intravenous bolus injection and continuous intravenous infusion.

25-mg, 5-mL vial—each sterile vial contains 25 mg diltiazem hydrochloride, 3.75 mg citric acid USP, 3.25 mg sodium citrate dihydrate USP, 357 mg sorbitol solution USP, and water for injection USP up to 5 mL. Sodium hydroxide or hydrochloric acid is used for pH adjustment.

50-mg, 10-mL vial—each sterile vial contains 50 mg diltiazem hydrochloride, 7.5 mg citric acid USP, 6.5 mg sodium citrate dihydrate USP, 714 mg sorbitol solution USP, and water for injection USP up to 10 mL. Sodium hydroxide or hydrochloric acid is used for pH adjustment.

CLINICAL PHARMACOLOGY

Mechanisms of Action. CARDIZEM inhibits the influx of calcium (CA^{2+}) ions during membrane depolarization of cardiac and vascular smooth muscle. The therapeutic benefits of CARDIZEM in supraventricular tachycardias are related to its ability to slow AV nodal conduction time and prolong AV nodal refractoriness. CARDIZEM exhibits frequency (use) dependent effects on AV nodal conduction such that it may selectively reduce the heart rate during tachycardias involving the AV node with little or no effect on normal AV nodal conduction at normal heart rates.

CARDIZEM slows the ventricular rate in patients with a rapid ventricular response during atrial fibrillation or atrial flutter. CARDIZEM converts paroxysmal supraventricular tachycardia (PSVT) to normal sinus rhythm by interrupting the reentry circuit in AV nodal reentrant tachycardias and reciprocating tachycardias, eg, Wolff-Parkinson-White syndrome (WPW).

CARDIZEM prolongs the sinus cycle length. It has no effect on the sinus node recovery time or on the sinoatrial conduction time in patients without SA nodal dysfunction. CARDIZEM has no significant electrophysiologic effect on tissues in the heart that are fast sodium channel dependent, eg, His-Purkinje tissue, atrial and ventricular muscle, and extranodal accessory pathways.

Like other calcium channel antagonists, because of its effect on vascular smooth muscle, CARDIZEM decreases total peripheral resistance resulting in a decrease in both systolic and diastolic blood pressure.

Hemodynamics. In patients with cardiovascular disease, CARDIZEM Injectable (diltiazem hydrochloride) administered intravenously in single bolus doses, followed in some cases by a continuous infusion, reduced blood pressure, systemic vascular resistance, the rate-pressure product, and coronary vascular resistance and increased coronary blood flow. In a limited number of studies of patients with compromised myocardium (severe congestive heart failure, acute myocardial infarction, hypertrophic cardiomyopathy), administration of intravenous diltiazem produced no significant effect on contractility, left ventricular end diastolic pressure, or pulmonary capillary wedge pressure. The mean ejection fraction and cardiac output/index remained unchanged or increased. Maximal hemodynamic effects usually occurred within 2 to 5 minutes of an injection. However, in rare instances, worsening of congestive heart failure has been reported in patients with preexisting impaired ventricular function.

Pharmacodynamics. The prolongation of PR interval correlated significantly with plasma diltiazem concentration in normal volunteers using the Sigmoidal E_{max} model. Changes in heart rate, systolic blood pressure, and diastolic blood pressure did not correlate with diltiazem plasma concentrations in normal volunteers. Reduction in mean arterial pressure correlated linearly with diltiazem plasma concentration in a group of hypertensive patients.

In patients with atrial fibrillation and atrial flutter, a significant correlation was observed between the percent reduction in HR and plasma diltiazem concentration using the Sigmoidal E_{max} model. Based on this relationship, the mean plasma diltiazem concentration required to produce a 20% decrease in heart rate was determined to be 80 ng/mL. Mean plasma diltiazem concentrations of 130 ng/mL and 300 ng/mL were determined to produce reductions in heart rate of 30% and 40%.

Pharmacokinetics and Metabolism. Following a single intravenous injection in healthy male volunteers, CARDIZEM appears to obey linear pharmacokinetics over a dose range of 10.5 to 21.0 mg. The plasma elimination half-life is approximately 3.4 hours. The apparent volume of distribution of CARDIZEM is approximately 305 L. CARDIZEM is extensively metabolized in the liver with a systemic clearance of approximately 65 L/h.

After constant rate intravenous infusion to healthy male volunteers, diltiazem exhibits nonlinear pharmacokinetics over an infusion range of 4.8 to 13.2 mg/h for 24 hours. Over this infusion range, as the dose is increased, systemic clearance decreases from 64 to 48 L/h while the plasma elimination half-life increases from 4.1 to 4.9 hours. The apparent volume of distribution remains unchanged (360 to 391 L). In patients with atrial fibrillation or atrial flutter, diltiazem systemic clearance has been found to be decreased compared to healthy volunteers. In patients administered bolus doses ranging from 2.5 mg to 38.5 mg, systemic clearance averaged 36 L/h. In patients administered continuous infusions at 10 mg/h or 15 mg/h for 24 hours, diltiazem systemic clearance averaged 42 L/h and 31 L/h, respectively.

Based on the results of pharmacokinetic studies in healthy volunteers administered different *oral* CARDIZEM formulations, constant rate intravenous infusions of CARDIZEM at 3, 5, 7, and 11 mg/h are predicted to produce steady-state plasma diltiazem concentrations equivalent to 120-, 180-, 240-, and 360-mg total daily oral doses of CARDIZEM tablets or CARDIZEM SR capsules.

After oral administration, CARDIZEM undergoes extensive metabolism in man by deacetylation, N-demethylation, and O-demethylation via cytochrome P-450 (oxidative metabolism) in addition to conjugation. Metabolites N-monodesmethyldiltiazem, desacetyldiltiazem, desacetyl-N-monodesmethyldiltiazem, desacetyl-O-desmethyldiltiazem, and desacetyl-N, O-desmethyldiltiazem have been identified in human urine. Following oral administration, 2% to 4% of the unchanged CARDIZEM appears in the urine. Drugs which induce or inhibit hepatic microsomal enzymes may alter diltiazem disposition.

Following single intravenous injection of CARDIZEM, however, plasma concentrations of N-monodesmethyldiltiazem and desacetyldiltiazem, two principal metabolites found in plasma after oral administration, are typically not detected. These metabolites are observed, however, following 24 hour constant rate intravenous infusion. Total radioactivity measurement following short IV administration in healthy volunteers suggests the presence of other unidentified metabolites which attain higher concentrations than those of diltiazem and are more slowly eliminated; half-life of total radioactivity is about 20 hours compared to 2 to 5 hours for diltiazem.

CARDIZEM is 70% to 80% bound to plasma proteins. In vitro studies suggest alpha$_1$-acid glycoprotein binds approximately 40% of the drug at clinically significant concentrations. Albumin appears to bind approximately 30% of the drug, while other constituents bind the remaining bound fraction. Competitive in vitro ligand binding studies have shown that CARDIZEM binding is not altered by therapeutic concentrations of digoxin, phenytoin, hydrochlorothiazide, indomethacin, phenylbutazone, propranolol, salicylic acid, tolbutamide, or warfarin.

Renal insufficiency, or even end-stage renal disease, does not appear to influence diltiazem disposition following *oral* administration. Liver cirrhosis was shown to reduce diltiazem apparent *oral* clearance and prolong its half-life.

INDICATIONS AND USAGE

CARDIZEM Injectable (diltiazem hydrochloride) is indicated for the following:

1. **Atrial Fibrillation or Atrial Flutter.** Temporary control of rapid ventricular rate in atrial fibrillation or atrial flutter. It should not be used in patients with atrial fibrillation or atrial flutter associated with an accessory bypass tract such as in Wolff-Parkinson-White (WPW) syndrome or short PR syndrome.

2. **Paroxysmal Supraventricular Tachycardia.** Rapid conversion of paroxysmal supraventricular tachycardias (PSVT) to sinus rhythm. This includes AV nodal reentrant tachycardias and reciprocating tachycardias associated with an extranodal accessory pathway such as the WPW syndrome or short PR syndrome. Unless otherwise contraindicated, appropriate vagal maneuvers should be attempted prior to administration of CARDIZEM Injectable.

The use of CARDIZEM Injectable for control of ventricular response in patients with atrial fibrillation or atrial flutter or conversion to sinus rhythm in patients with PSVT should be undertaken with caution when the patient is compromised hemodynamically or is taking other drugs that decrease any or all of the following: peripheral resistance, myocardial filling, myocardial contractility, or electrical impulse propagation in the myocardium.

For either indication and particularly when employing continuous intravenous infusion, the setting should include continuous monitoring of the ECG and frequent measurement of blood pressure. A defibrillator and emergency equipment should be readily available.

In domestic controlled trials in patients with atrial fibrillation or atrial flutter, bolus administration of CARDIZEM Injectable was effective in reducing heart rate by at least 20% in 95% of patients. CARDIZEM Injectable rarely converts atrial fibrillation or atrial flutter to normal sinus rhythm. Following administration of one or two intravenous bolus doses of CARDIZEM Injectable, response usually occurs within 3 minutes and maximal heart rate reduction generally occurs in 2 to 7 minutes. Heart rate reduction may last from 1 to 3 hours. If hypotension occurs, it is generally short-lived, but may last from 1 to 3 hours.

A 24-hour continuous infusion of CARDIZEM Injectable in the treatment of atrial fibrillation or atrial flutter maintained at least a 20% heart rate reduction during the infusion in 83% of patients. Upon discontinuation of infusion, heart rate reduction may last from 0.5 hours to more than 10 hours (median duration 7 hours). Hypotension, if it occurs, may be similarly persistent.

In the controlled clinical trials, 3.2% of patients required some form of intervention (typically, use of intravenous fluids or the Trendelenburg position) for blood pressure support following CARDIZEM Injectable.

In domestic controlled trials, bolus administration of CARDIZEM Injectable was effective in converting PSVT to normal sinus rhythm in 88% of patients within 3 minutes of the first or second bolus dose.

Symptoms associated with the arrhythmia were improved in conjunction with decreased heart rate or conversion to normal sinus rhythm following administration of CARDIZEM Injectable.

CONTRAINDICATIONS

CARDIZEM Injectable is contraindicated in:

1. Patients with sick sinus syndrome except in the presence of a functioning ventricular pacemaker.

2. Patients with second- or third-degree AV block except in the presence of a functioning ventricular pacemaker.

3. Patients with severe hypotension or cardiogenic shock.

4. Patients who have demonstrated hypersensitivity to the drug.

5. Intravenous diltiazem and intravenous beta-blockers should not be administered together or in close proximity (within a few hours).

6. Patients with atrial fibrillation or atrial flutter associated with an accessory bypass tract such as in WPW syndrome or short PR syndrome.

   As with other agents which slow AV nodal conduction and do not prolong the refractoriness of the accessory pathway (eg, verapamil, digoxin), in rare instances patients in atrial fibrillation or atrial flutter associated with an accessory bypass tract may experience a potentially life-threatening increase in heart rate accompanied by hypotension when treated with CARDIZEM Injectable. As such, the initial use of CARDIZEM Injectable should be, if possible, in a setting where monitoring and resuscitation capabilities, including DC cardioversion/defibrillation, are present (see OVERDOSAGE). Once familiarity of the patient's response is established, use in an office setting may be acceptable.

7. Patients with ventricular tachycardia. Administration of other calcium channel blockers to patients with wide complex tachycardia (QRS ≥ 0.12 seconds) has resulted in hemodynamic deterioration and ventricular fibrillation. It is important that an accurate pretreatment diagnosis distinguish wide complex QRS tachycardia of supraventricular origin from that of ventricular origin prior to administration of CARDIZEM Injectable.

WARNINGS

1. **Cardiac Conduction.** Diltiazem prolongs AV nodal conduction and refractoriness that may rarely result in second- or third-degree AV block in sinus rhythm. Concomitant use of diltiazem with agents known to affect cardiac conduction may result in additive effects (see Drug Interactions). If high-degree AV block occurs in sinus rhythm, intravenous diltiazem should be discontinued and appropriate supportive measures instituted (see OVERDOSAGE).

2. **Congestive Heart Failure.** Although diltiazem has a negative inotropic effect in isolated animal tissue preparations, hemodynamic studies in humans with normal ventricular function and in patients with a compromised myocardium, such as severe CHF, acute MI, and hypertrophic cardiomyopathy, have not shown a reduction in cardiac index nor consistent negative effects on contractility (dp/dt). Administration of oral diltiazem in patients with acute myocardial infarction and pulmonary congestion documented by x-ray on admission is contraindicated. Experience with the use of

CARDIZEM Injectable in patients with impaired ventricular function is limited. Caution should be exercised when using the drug in such patients.

3. **Hypotension.** Decreases in blood pressure associated with CARDIZEM Injectable therapy may occasionally result in symptomatic hypotension (3.2%). The use of intravenous diltiazem for control of ventricular response in patients with supraventricular arrhythmias should be undertaken with caution when the patient is compromised hemodynamically. In addition, caution should be used in patients taking other drugs that decrease peripheral resistance, intravascular volume, myocardial contractility or conduction.

4. **Acute Hepatic Injury.** In rare instances, significant elevations in enzymes such as alkaline phosphatase, LDH, SGOT, SGPT, and other phenomena consistent with acute hepatic injury have been noted following oral diltiazem. Therefore, the potential for acute hepatic injury exists following administration of intravenous diltiazem.

5. **Ventricular Premature Beats (VPBs).** VPBs may be present on conversion of PSVT to sinus rhythm with CARDIZEM Injectable. These VPBs are transient, are typically considered to be benign, and appear to have no clinical significance. Similar ventricular complexes have been noted during cardioversion, other pharmacologic therapy, and during spontaneous conversion of PSVT to sinus rhythm.

PRECAUTIONS

General. CARDIZEM (diltiazem hydrochloride) is extensively metabolized by the liver and excreted by the kidneys and in bile. The drug should be used with caution in patients with impaired renal or hepatic function (see WARNINGS). High intravenous dosages (4.5 mg/kg tid) administered to dogs resulted in significant bradycardia and alterations in AV conduction. In subacute and chronic dog and rat studies designed to produce toxicity, high oral doses of diltiazem were associated with hepatic damage. In special subacute hepatic studies, oral doses of 125 mg/kg and higher in rats were associated with histological changes in the liver, which were reversible when the drug was discontinued. In dogs, oral doses of 20 mg/kg were also associated with hepatic changes; however, these changes were reversible with continued dosing.

Dermatologic events progressing to erythema multiforme and/or exfoliative dermatitis have been infrequently reported following oral diltiazem. Therefore, the potential for these dermatologic reactions exists following exposure to intravenous diltiazem. Should a dermatologic reaction persist, the drug should be discontinued.

Drug Interactions. Due to potential for additive effects, caution is warranted in patients receiving CARDIZEM Injectable concomitantly with any agent(s) known to affect cardiac contractility and/or SA or AV node conduction (see WARNINGS).

As with all drugs, care should be exercised when treating patients with multiple medications. CARDIZEM undergoes extensive metabolism by the cytochrome P-450 mixed function oxidase system. Although specific pharmacokinetic drug-drug interaction studies have not been conducted with single intravenous injection or constant rate intravenous infusion, coadministration of CARDIZEM Injectable with other agents which primarily undergo the same route of biotransformation may result in competitive inhibition of metabolism.

Digitalis: Intravenous diltiazem has been administered to patients receiving either intravenous or oral digitalis therapy. The combination of the two drugs was well tolerated without serious adverse effects. However, since both drugs affect AV nodal conduction, patients should be monitored for excessive slowing of the heart rate and/or AV block.

Beta-blockers: Intravenous diltiazem has been administered to patients on chronic oral beta-blocker therapy. The combination of the two drugs is generally well tolerated without serious adverse effects. If intravenous diltiazem is administered to patients receiving chronic oral beta-blocker therapy, the possibility for bradycardia, AV block, and/or depression of contractility should be considered (see CONTRAINDICATIONS). *Oral* administration of diltiazem with propranolol in five normal volunteers resulted in increased propranolol levels in all subjects and bioavailability of propranolol was increased approximately 50%. In vitro, propranolol appears to be displaced from its binding sites by diltiazem.

Anesthetics: The depression of cardiac contractility, conductivity, and automaticity as well as the vascular dilation associated with anesthetics may be potentiated by calcium channel blockers. When used concomitantly, anesthetics and calcium blockers should be titrated carefully.

Carcinogenesis, Mutagenesis, Impairment of Fertility. A 24-month study in rats at oral dosage levels of up to 100 mg/kg/day, and a 21-month study in mice at oral dosage levels of up to 30 mg/kg/day showed no evidence of carcinogenicity. There was also no mutagenic response in vitro or in vivo in mammalian cell assays or in vitro in bacteria. No evidence of impaired fertility was observed in a study performed in male and female rats at oral dosages of up to 100 mg/kg/day.

Pregnancy. Category C. Reproduction studies have been conducted in mice, rats, and rabbits. Administration of oral doses ranging from five to ten times greater (on a mg/kg basis) than the daily recommended oral antianginal therapeutic dose has resulted in embryo and fetal lethality. These doses, in some studies, have been reported to cause skeletal abnormalities. In the perinatal/postnatal studies there was some reduction in early individual pup weights and survival rates. There was an increased incidence of stillbirths at doses of 20 times the human oral antianginal dose or greater.

There are no well-controlled studies in pregnant women; therefore, use CARDIZEM in pregnant women only if the potential benefit justifies the potential risk to the fetus.

Nursing Mothers. Diltiazem is excreted in human milk. One report with oral diltiazem suggests that concentrations in breast milk may approximate serum levels. If use of CARDIZEM is deemed essential, an alternative method of infant feeding should be instituted.

Pediatric Use. Safety and effectiveness in children have not been established.

ADVERSE REACTIONS

The following adverse reaction rates are based on the use of CARDIZEM Injectable in over 400 domestic clinical trial patients with atrial fibrillation/flutter or PSVT under double-blind or open-label conditions. Worldwide experience in over 1,300 patients was similar.

Adverse events reported in controlled and uncontrolled clinical trials were generally mild and transient. Hypotension was the most commonly reported adverse event during clinical trials. Asymptomatic hypotension occurred in 4.3% of patients. Symptomatic hypotension occurred in 3.2% of patients. When treatment for hypotension was required, it generally consisted of administration of saline or placing the patient in the Trendelenburg position. Other events reported in at least 1% of the diltiazem-treated patients were injection site reactions (eg, itching, burning)—3.9%, vasodilation (flushing)—1.7%, and arrhythmia (junctional rhythm or isorhythmic dissociation)—1.0%.

In addition, the following events were reported infrequently (less than 1%):

Cardiovascular:	Atrial flutter, AV block first degree, AV block second degree, bradycardia, chest pain, congestive heart failure, sinus pause, sinus node dysfunction, syncope, ventricular arrhythmia, ventricular fibrillation, ventricular tachycardia.
Dermatologic:	Pruritus, sweating.
Gastrointestinal:	Constipation, elevated SGOT or alkaline phosphatase, nausea, vomiting.
Nervous System:	Dizziness, paresthesia.
Other:	Amblyopia, asthenia, dry mouth, dyspnea, edema, headache, hyperuricemia.

Although not observed in clinical trials with CARDIZEM Injectable, other reactions associated with oral diltiazem may occur.

OVERDOSAGE

Overdosage experience is limited. In the event of overdosage or an exaggerated response, appropriate supportive measures should be employed. The following measures may be considered:

Bradycardia:	Administer atropine (0.60 to 1.0 mg). If there is no response to vagal blockade administer isoproterenol cautiously.
High-degree AV Block:	Treat as for bradycardia above. Fixed high-degree AV block should be treated with cardiac pacing.
Cardiac Failure:	Administer inotropic agents (isoproterenol, dopamine, or dobutamine) and diuretics.
Hypotension:	Vasopressors (eg, dopamine or levarterenol bitartrate).

Actual treatment and dosage should depend on the severity of the clinical situation and the judgment and experience of the treating physician.

The intravenous LD_{50}'s in mice and rats were 60 and 38 mg/kg, respectively. The toxic dose in man is not known.

DOSAGE AND ADMINISTRATION

Direct Intravenous Single Injections (Bolus)
The initial dose of CARDIZEM Injectable should be 0.25 mg/kg actual body weight as a bolus administered over 2 minutes (20 mg is a reasonable dose for the average patient). If response is inadequate, a second dose may be administered after 15 minutes. The second bolus dose of CARDIZEM Injectable should be 0.35 mg/kg actual body weight administered over 2 minutes (25 mg is a reasonable dose for the average patient). Subsequent intravenous bolus doses should be individualized for each patient. Patients with low body weights should be dosed on a mg/kg basis. Some patients may respond to an initial dose of 0.15 mg/kg, although duration of action may be shorter. Experience with this dose is limited.

Continuous Intravenous Infusion
For continued reduction of the heart rate (up to 24 hours) in patients with atrial fibrillation or atrial flutter, an intravenous infusion of CARDIZEM Injectable may be administered. Immediately following bolus administration of 20 mg (0.25 mg/kg) or 25 mg (0.35 mg/kg) CARDIZEM Injectable and reduction of heart rate, begin an intravenous infusion of CARDIZEM Injectable. The recommended initial infusion rate of CARDIZEM Injectable is 10 mg/h. Some patients may maintain response to an initial rate of 5 mg/h. The infusion rate may be increased in 5 mg/h increments up to 15 mg/h as needed, if further reduction in heart rate is required. The infusion may be maintained for up to 24 hours.

Diltiazem shows dose-dependent, non-linear pharmacokinetics. Duration of infusion longer than 24 hours and infusion rates greater than 15 mg/h have not been studied. Therefore, infusion duration exceeding 24 hours and infusion rates exceeding 15 mg/h are not recommended.

Dilution: To prepare CARDIZEM Injectable for continuous intravenous infusion aseptically transfer the appropriate quantity (see chart) of CARDIZEM Injectable to the desired volume of either Normal Saline, D5W, or D5W/0.45% NaCl. Mix thoroughly. Use within 24 hours. Keep refrigerated until use.

Diluent Volume	Quantity of Cardizem Injection	Final Concentration	Administration	
			Dose*	Infusion Rate
100 mL	125 mg (25 mL)	1.0 mg/mL	10 mg/h 15 mg/h	10 mL/h 15 mL/h
250 mL	250 mg (50 mL)	0.83 mg/mL	10 mg/h 15 mg/h	12 mL/h 18 mL/h
500 mL	250 mg (50 mL)	0.45 mg/mL	10 mg/h 15 mg/h	22 mL/h 33 mL/h

* 5 mg/h may be appropriate for some patients

CARDIZEM Injectable was tested for compatibility with three commonly used intravenous fluids at a maximal concentration of 1 mg diltiazem hydrochloride per milliliter. CARDIZEM Injectable was found to be physically compatible and chemically stable in the following parenteral solutions for at least 24 hours when stored in glass or polyvinylchloride (PVC) bags at controlled room temperature 15-30°C (59-86°F) or under refrigeration 2-8°C (36-46°F).

• dextrose (5%) injection USP
• sodium chloride (0.9%) injection USP
• dextrose (5%) and sodium chloride (0.45%) injection USP.

CARDIZEM Injectable is incompatible when mixed directly with furosemide solution.

Parenteral drug products should be inspected visually for particulate matter and discoloration prior to administration whenever solution and container permit.

Transition to Further Antiarrhythmic Therapy. Transition to other antiarrhythmic agents following administration of CARDIZEM Injectable is generally safe. However, reference should be made to the respective agent manufacturer's package insert for information relative to dosage and administration.

In controlled clinical trials, therapy with antiarrhythmic agents to maintain reduced heart rate in atrial fibrillation or atrial flutter or for prophylaxis of PSVT was generally started within 3 hours after bolus administration of CARDIZEM Injectable. These antiarrhythmic agents were intravenous or oral digoxin, Class I antiarrhythmics (eg, quinidine, procainamide), calcium channel blockers, and oral beta-blockers.

Experience in the use of antiarrhythmic agents following maintenance infusion of CARDIZEM Injectable is limited. Patients should be dosed on an individual basis and reference should be made to the respective manufacturer's package insert for information relative to dosage and administration.

HOW SUPPLIED

CARDIZEM® Injectable (diltiazem hydrochloride injection) is supplied in boxes of six 5-mL vials with each vial containing 25 mg of diltiazem hydrochloride (5 mg/mL) (NDC 0088-1790-32) and boxes of six 10-mL vials with each vial containing 50 mg diltiazem hydrochloride (5 mg/mL) (NDC 0088-1790-33).

SINGLE-USE CONTAINERS. DISCARD UNUSED PORTION.

STORE PRODUCT UNDER REFRIGERATION 2°-8°C (36°-46°F). DO NOT FREEZE. MAY BE STORED AT ROOM TEMPERATURE FOR UP TO 1 MONTH. DESTROY AFTER 1 MONTH AT ROOM TEMPERATURE.

Product information as of October 1991

MARION MERRELL DOW INC.
PRESCRIPTION PRODUCTS DIVISION
KANSAS CITY, MO 64114

CARAFATE® Tablets
(sucralfate)

DESCRIPTION
CARAFATE (sucralfate) is an α-D-glucopyranoside, β-D-fructofuranosyl-, octakis-(hydrogen sulfate), aluminum complex.

$$R = SO_3[Al_2 (OH)_5 \cdot (H_2O)_2]$$

Tablets for oral administration contain 1 gm of sucralfate.
Also contain: D&C Red # 30 Lake, FD&C Blue # 1 Lake, magnesium stearate, microcrystalline cellulose, and starch.
Therapeutic category: antiulcer.

CLINICAL PHARMACOLOGY
Sucralfate is only minimally absorbed from the gastrointestinal tract. The small amounts of the sulfated disaccharide that are absorbed are excreted primarily in the urine.
Although the mechanism of sucralfate's ability to accelerate healing of duodenal ulcers remains to be fully defined, it is known that it exerts its effect through a local, rather than systemic, action. The following observations also appear pertinent:

1. Studies in human subjects and with animal models of ulcer disease have shown that sucralfate forms an ulcer-adherent complex with proteinaceous exudate at the ulcer site.
2. In vitro, a sucralfate-albumin film provides a barrier to diffusion of hydrogen ions.
3. In human subjects, sucralfate given in doses recommended for ulcer therapy inhibits pepsin activity in gastric juice by 32%.
4. In vitro, sucralfate adsorbs bile salts.

These observations suggest that sucralfate's antiulcer activity is the result of formation of an ulcer-adherent complex that covers the ulcer site and protects it against further attack by acid, pepsin, and bile salts. There are approximately 14-16 mEq of acid-neutralizing capacity per 1-gm dose of sucralfate.

CLINICAL TRIALS
Acute Duodenal Ulcer
Over 600 patients have participated in well-controlled clinical trials worldwide. Multicenter trials conducted in the United States, both of them placebo-controlled studies with endoscopic evaluation at 2 and 4 weeks, showed:

STUDY 1		
Treatment Groups	Ulcer Healing/No. Patients	
	2 wk	4 wk (Overall)
Sucralfate	37/105 (35.2%)	82/109 (75.2%)
Placebo	26/106 (24.5%)	68/107 (63.6%)

STUDY 2		
Treatment Groups	Ulcer Healing/No. Patients	
	2 wk	4 wk (Overall)
Sucralfate	8/24 (33%)	22/24 (92%)
Placebo	4/31 (13%)	18/31 (58%)

The sucralfate-placebo differences were statistically significant in both studies at 4 weeks but not at 2 weeks. The poorer result in the first study may have occurred because sucralfate was given 2 hours after meals and at bedtime rather than 1 hour before meals and at bedtime, the regimen used in international studies and in the second United States study. In addition, in the first study liquid antacid was utilized as needed, whereas in the second study antacid tablets were used.

Maintenance Therapy After Healing of Duodenal Ulcer
Two double-blind randomized placebo-controlled U.S. multicenter trials have demonstrated that sucralfate (1 gm bid) is effective as maintenance therapy following healing of duodenal ulcers.
In one study, endoscopies were performed monthly for 4 months. Of the 254 patients who enrolled, 239 were analyzed in the intention-to-treat life table analysis presented below.

Duodenal Ulcer Recurrence Rate (%)					
		Months of Therapy			
Drug	N	1	2	3	4
CARAFATE	122	20*	30*	38**	42**
Placebo	117	33	46	55	63

*p<0.05, **p<0.01
Prn antacids were not permitted in this study.

In the other study, scheduled endoscopies were performed at 6 and 12 months, but for cause endoscopies were permitted as symptoms dictated. Median symptom scores between the sucralfate and placebo groups were not significantly different. A life table intention-to-treat analysis for the 94 patients enrolled in the trial had the following results:

Duodenal Ulcer Recurrence Rate (%)			
Drug	N	6 months	12 months
CARAFATE	48	19*	27*
Placebo	46	54	65

*p<0.002
Prn antacids were permitted in this study.
Data from placebo-controlled studies longer than 1 year are not available.

INDICATIONS AND USAGE
CARAFATE® (sucralfate) is indicated in:
- Short-term treatment (up to 8 weeks) of active duodenal ulcer. While healing with sucralfate may occur during the first week or two, treatment should be continued for 4 to 8 weeks unless healing has been demonstrated by x-ray or endoscopic examination.
- Maintenance therapy for duodenal ulcer patients at reduced dosage after healing of acute ulcers.

CONTRAINDICATIONS
There are no known contraindications to the use of sucralfate.

PRECAUTIONS
Duodenal ulcer is a chronic, recurrent disease. While short-term treatment with sucralfate can result in complete healing of the ulcer, a successful course of treatment with sucralfate should not be expected to alter the posthealing frequency or severity of duodenal ulceration.

Special Populations: Chronic Renal Failure and Dialysis Patients
When sucralfate is administered orally, small amounts of aluminum are absorbed from the gastrointestinal tract. Concomitant use of sucralfate with other products that contain aluminum, such as aluminum-containing antacids, may increase the total body burden of aluminum. Patients with normal renal function receiving the recommended doses of sucralfate and aluminum-containing products adequately excrete aluminum in the urine. Patients with chronic renal failure or those receiving dialysis have impaired excretion of absorbed aluminum. In addition, aluminum does not cross dialysis membranes because it is bound to albumin and transferrin plasma proteins. Aluminum accumulation and toxicity (aluminum osteodystrophy, osteomalacia, encephalopathy) have been described in patients with renal impairment. Sucralfate should be used with caution in patients with chronic renal failure.

Drug Interactions
Some studies have shown that simultaneous sucralfate administration in healthy volunteers reduced the extent of absorption (bioavailability) of single doses of the following drugs: cimetidine, ciprofloxacin, digoxin, ketoconazole, norfloxacin, phenytoin, ranitidine, tetracycline, and theophylline. Subtherapeutic prothrombin times with concomitant warfarin and sucralfate therapy have been reported in spontaneous and published case reports. However, two clinical studies have demonstrated no change in either serum warfarin concentration or prothrombin time with the addition of sucralfate to chronic warfarin therapy.
The mechanism of these interactions appears to be nonsystemic in nature, presumably resulting from sucralfate binding to the concomitant agent in the gastrointestinal tract. In all cases studied to date (cimetidine, ciprofloxacin, digoxin, ranitidine, and warfarin), dosing the concomitant medication 2 hours before sucralfate eliminated the interaction. Because of the potential of CARAFATE to alter the absorption of some drugs, CARAFATE should be administered separately from other drugs when alterations in bioavailability are felt to be critical. In these cases, patients should be monitored appropriately.

Carcinogenesis, Mutagenesis, Impairment of Fertility
Chronic oral toxicity studies of 24 months' duration were conducted in mice and rats at doses up to 1 gm/kg (12 times the human dose). There was no evidence of drug-related tumorigenicity. A reproduction study in rats at doses up to 38 times the human dose did not reveal any indication of fertility impairment. Mutagenicity studies were not conducted.

Pregnancy
Teratogenic effects. Pregnancy Category B. Teratogenicity studies have been performed in mice, rats, and rabbits at doses up to 50 times the human dose and have revealed no evidence of harm to the fetus due to sucralfate. There are, however, no adequate and well-controlled studies in pregnant women. Because animal reproduction studies are not always predictive of human response, this drug should be used during pregnancy only if clearly needed.

Nursing Mothers
It is not known whether this drug is excreted in human milk. Because many drugs are excreted in human milk, caution should be exercised when sucralfate is administered to a nursing woman.

Pediatric Use
Safety and effectiveness in children have not been established.

ADVERSE REACTIONS
Adverse reactions to sucralfate in clinical trials were minor and only rarely led to discontinuation of the drug. In studies involving over 2700 patients treated with sucralfate tablets, adverse effects were reported in 129 (4.7%).
Constipation was the most frequent complaint (2%). Other adverse effects reported in less than 0.5% of the patients are listed below by body system:
Gastrointestinal: diarrhea, nausea, vomiting, gastric discomfort, indigestion, flatulence, dry mouth
Dermatological: pruritus, rash
Nervous System: dizziness, insomnia, sleepiness, vertigo
Other: back pain, headache

Postmarketing reports of hypersensitivity reactions, including urticaria (hives), angioedema, respiratory difficulty, and rhinitis have been received. However, a causal relationship has not been established.

OVERDOSAGE

There is no experience in humans with overdosage. Acute oral toxicity studies in animals, however, using doses up to 12 gm/kg body weight, could not find a lethal dose. Risks associated with overdosage should, therefore, be minimal.

DOSAGE AND ADMINISTRATION

Active Duodenal Ulcer: The recommended adult oral dosage for duodenal ulcer is 1 gm four times a day on an empty stomach.

Antacids may be prescribed as needed for relief of pain but should not be taken within one-half hour before or after sucralfate.

While healing with sucralfate may occur during the first week or two, treatment should be continued for 4 to 8 weeks unless healing has been demonstrated by x-ray or endoscopic examination.

Maintenance Therapy: The recommended adult oral dosage is 1 gm twice a day.

HOW SUPPLIED

CARAFATE (sucralfate) 1-gm tablets are supplied in bottles of 100 (NDC 0088-1712-47), 120 (NDC 0088-1712-53), and 500 (NDC 0088-1712-55) and in Unit Dose Identification Paks of 100 (NDC 0088-1712-49). Light pink scored oblong tablets are embossed with CARAFATE on one side and 1712 on the other.

Prescribing Information as of October 1992

Marion Merrell Dow Inc.
Kansas City, MO 64114

cafp1092f